Self-Guided Tour

THE BATTLE OF
NEW MARKET

Joseph W. A. Whitehorne

Center of Military History
United States Army
Washington, D.C., 1988

Library of Congress Cataloging-in-Publication Data

Whitehorne, Joseph W. A., 1943-
  The Battle of New Market.

  (CMH pub ; 70-24)
  1. New Market, Battle of, 1864. 2. Historic sites—
Virginia—New Market Region—Guide—books. 3. New
Market Region (Va.)—Description and travel—Guide-books.
I. Title. II. Series.
E476.64.W46 1988   917.55'95   88-34357

Illustrations unless fully identified under the photo are from the following sources: Edward R. Turner, *The New Market Campaign, 1864,* Richmond, Va.: Whittet & Sheppson, 1912; Francis T. Miller, *The Photographic History of the Civil War*, New York: Review of Reviews, 1911; John W. Wayland, *Stonewall Jackson's Way*, Verona, Va.: The McClure Printing Co., 1940; the National Archives and Records Administration (NARA); the Military History Institute; and the U.S. Military Academy. Maps were drawn by John R. Treibor.

First Printing—CMH Pub. 70–24

For sale by the Superintendent of Documents, U.S. Government Printing Office
Washington, D.C. 20402

Foreword

The visitor to this battlefield will learn that it has been preserved and developed in relatively recent times. It has, however, been an object of interest and reverence almost since the moment the battle ended. The participation of the Virginia Military Institute (VMI) cadets and the success of the other Virginia troops in defending their homes give the battle an added poignancy; the endurance, courage, and dedication of the Federals can be an equal source of pride. We of the profession of arms need places like this to renew our own dedication and to deepen our understanding and appreciation for our predecessors' skills as practitioners of the art and science of war. The military profession must continue to learn from the past to be ready for its future. In accordance with this need, the Center of Military History is producing a series of staff ride brochures, of which this is the first.

Washington, D.C.
1 August 1988

WILLIAM A. STOFFT
Brigadier General, USA
Chief of Military History

Introduction

The Battle of New Market was the first of a series of engagements taking place in the summer and fall of 1864 that destroyed Confederate power in the Shenandoah Valley. This first battle hardly presaged such an outcome. It was waged between two provisional field organizations hastily assembled by their respective commanders days before contact. Confederate success in the face of greater odds seemed to be a repetition of the days of Stonewall Jackson. Just as in those days of 1862, this was the result of able leadership characterized by a clear vision of the strategic and tactical situation, agility, and synchronization. The Federal defeat can be attributed to the reverse of these principles. Federal strength was frittered away in a series of doctrinaire decisions devoid of reality. Unit cohesiveness was disregarded, and forces were committed with little concept of the Federal objectives or the tactical situation. The battle may be summarized as a Federal movement to contact, Confederate defense and counterattack, and a hasty Federal withdrawal.

Following a general briefing, this tour will go to twelve locations important to aspects of the battle. The first part of the tour will be by vehicle, while the remainder will be on foot. The approximately two miles of walking will be in the confines of the Virginia Military Institute battlefield park on roads and open field. Ground can be marshy in places after rain. Field glasses would be useful at several stops. The tour will conclude with a visit to the battlefield museum.

Rarely has a battle demonstrated the virtues and defects of opposing commanders so clearly. The quality of the units on either side was never in question. Understanding the battle's outcome provides valuable insight into leadership, cohesiveness, and the operational art.

The following "Overview" should be read before taking the tour. Stops are keyed to the action described in the overview. Numbered stops are those made by car. "CR" indicates County Road. Stops with numbers and letters are optional additions to the motor phase of the tour. Stops with letters alone are those made walking on the battlefield. In the Overview names of Confederate personnel and units appear in italic type, Union personnel and units in regular type.

Washington, D.C.
1 August 1988

JOSEPH W. A. WHITEHORNE
Lieutenant Colonel
United States Army

Contents

Cover: *Charge of the VMI New Market Cadets* by Jack Woodson, courtesy of VMI.

Overview

Strategic Background

On 4 March 1864 *Maj. Gen. John C. Breckinridge* moved from Tennessee to take command of the Confederate Department of Western Virginia. This huge command consisted of nearly 18,000 square miles of rugged terrain. It included all of Virginia west of the Blue Ridge and south of Staunton; the southern part of modern West Virginia from Greenbriar County to Kentucky; and as much of the last state as was under Confederate control. The dynamic commander's mission was to defend along a 400-mile front to assure retention of the region's assets and resources for the Confederacy.

Breckinridge's district was of vital economic and strategic importance to the Confederate war effort. Wythe County at its center contained some of the largest lead mines in the South. Almost all the Confederacy's salt was produced in nearby Saltville. The upper Shenandoah Valley was a prime source of produce and livestock. These were essential to the sustenance of *Robert E. Lee's army* east of the Blue Ridge, poised to defend Richmond against an expected Federal onslaught. The region further contained important railroads running through Staunton or Lynchburg. The latter line, the Virginia and Tennessee, linked the two sections of the embattled Confederacy and were of great strategic significance. The presence of Federal raiders and a partially disaffected population compounded the difficulties in assuring the security of the district.

The point to which Confederate arms had declined by the spring of 1864 may be seen in *Breckinridge's* being given fewer than 5,000 troops to protect this important area. *Colonel John McCausland's Brigade*, 1,268 strong, was at New River Narrows while *Brig. Gen. John Echols* with 1,769 men was based at Monroe Draught. *Breckinridge* further inherited two poorly organized cavalry brigades with a combined strength of about 1,800. Two artillery batteries and a staff of couriers and signalers rounded out his forces. Other troops assigned to his command were on temporary duty elsewhere. Both *Brig. Gen. Gabriel C. Wharton's infantry brigade* and *Brig. Gen. W. E. "Grumble" Jones' cavalry brigade* were absent in Tennessee. One other unit, the *45th Virginia Infantry*, was at Saltville, but at first was not under *Breckinridge's* jurisdiction.

Undaunted, the vigorous commander immediately embarked upon a 400-mile tour of his district to assess the situation for himself. This was the first time such a tour had been carried out by any senior official and in itself was a tonic for his troops and sympathetic civilians. He recognized manpower as his first concern. Within two weeks he increased the number of effectives through better organization, reduction of details and furloughs, and enforcement of desertion and absent-without-leave policies. By the end of March, he was able to organize an additional cavalry brigade, which he placed under the command of *Brig. Gen. Albert Jenkins*. His tour allowed him to gain a first-hand

John C. Breckinridge (NARA)

impression of the geographic vulnerabilities of his district. He thus revised old defense plans and prepared contingencies to cover all the possible avenues of approach to the district's vitals. *Breckinridge's* description of the scope of the problems facing him persuaded *General Lee* to order the return of *Wharton's and Jones' brigades* to the district and the transfer of the *45th Virginia* to *Breckinridge's* control. He had these units in hand by mid-April, generally deployed to protect the assets of Wythe County.

The former politician worked to ease the tensions further between the government and the population. Richmond had become very high-handed in its procurement practices. The district commanders often had been directed to impress produce and goods with little compensation. Also, huge quantities had been sent east with little thought for the needs of *Breckinridge's* district. As a result, he often found hungry units amidst plenty, with many disenchanted farmers. He ended these practices by ordering fair requisitions and by telling Richmond that his district had priority before anything would be shipped out of it. This new policy marked another improvement in morale for the troops, while it stabilized relations with the civilian populace.

Breckinridge restored leadership and direction to his command just in time. He had barely returned to his headquarters in Dublin when he began to hear rumors of Federal activity. On 27 April he learned that a Federal column under Brig. Gen. William Averell was gathering at Logan, West Virginia, with the apparent intent of moving on Wytheville. Another Federal force was massing under Brig. Gen. George Crook at Gauley Bridge, West Virginia, which threatened to strike the Virginia and Tennessee Railroad near Dublin. A third Federal column was concentrating farther north at Martinsburg, West Virginia, under Maj. Gen. Franz Sigel, obviously preparing to move up the Valley. *Breckinridge* knew he had just a few days to assess the situation and to

Franz Sigel (MHI)

make the correct strategic decision. He had to determine the Federal intentions, identify the greatest threat, and deploy against it to achieve mass at the decisive point. Events were to prove that he made a masterful analysis.

Before discussing *Breckinridge's* decision, a view of the Federal moves in their greater context is necessary. All the blue forces just mentioned were under the command of Maj. Gen. Franz Sigel who had assumed command of the U.S. Department of West Virginia on 10 March. His department's mission was part of a Federal strategy developed by newly appointed General-in-Chief Ulysses S. Grant. General Grant recognized that superior Federal resources had not been used effectively hitherto and likened the Federal army to a balky team with each mule going in a different direction. He saw his job as getting that mule team to pull together.

One of Grant's aides described the situation as it was in March 1864: "Grant inherited mass confusion in the Federal command when we came to Washington. There were a score of discordant armies, half a score of contrary campaigns, confusion and uncertainty in the field, doubt and dejection and sometimes despondency at home. Battles whose object none could perceive, a war whose issues none could foretell. It was chaos itself."

An expression of this chaos was that at the time of Grant's assumption the Federals had 19 independent districts, 21 independent corps, and 1 independent army, along with 13 coastal enclaves working separately with the Navy. Grant said, "My primary mission is to achieve system and discipline and consolidate and coordinate these assets and to bring pressure to bear on the Confederacy so no longer could it take advantage of interior lines." Grant thus brought greater cohesiveness to the Northern war effort. He was the first Northern leader to be able to bring the Federal preponderance in strength to bear in a unified effort. He added new dimensions to the struggle by seeing the war as more than a simple military undertaking. He reasoned that in such a thing as an insurrection, the entire population in rebellion had to be persuaded of the folly of continuing the fight. To him the Southern ability and will to fight were as valid objectives as were the Confederate armies. He added economic, political, and psychological aspects to the war that hitherto had been missing. All of them revolved around his intentions to engineer a massive continental-scale assault to overwhelm the Confederacy. As he told Maj. Gen. George G. Meade, "All our armies are to move together toward one common center; and that is the destruction of the other's will to fight."

General Grant assigned General Meade's 100,000-man Army of the Potomac to attack *General Robert E. Lee's Army of Northern Virginia* in eastern Virginia, destroy it, and capture Richmond. Meade's force would serve also as the strategic hinge for a great pivot through Georgia by Maj. Gen. William T. Sherman's army group. Each of these units had military, economic, and psychological objectives. Their strategic flanks were to be protected by other forces: Major General Nathaniel Banks was to sally from New Orleans against Mobile Bay. In the east, Maj. Gen. Benjamin F. Butler's Army of the James was to move from Fort Monroe to Bermuda Hundred against Richmond. Meade's western flank was to be secured by Franz Sigel's activities in the Valley. Sigel was to coordinate Crook's and Averell's moves against the Virginia and Tennessee Railroad and Wytheville and to prevent Confederate reinforcements from reaching *Lee*. Further, Sigel planned to lead a force up the Valley to resupply the raiders and to draw off Confederates from the threatened area.

The Valley was as important to the Federals as it was to the Confederates. A corresponding communications system graced its northern parts. The Baltimore and Ohio Railroad and the Chesapeake and Ohio Canal were critically important strategic routes for the Federals. Huge efforts were expended throughout the war to provide security for them. The road net in the Valley was exceptionally good; it was based on the Valley Pike, macadamized since 1840, linked with an infrastructure of good secondary roads. Not only was the place a prosperous economic unit, but also its development accommodated high-speed movement. The Blue Ridge shielded the Valley from eastern Virginia; however, ample gaps allowed easy egress and entry. Its northeastern orientation made it a natural avenue of approach into Pennsylvania or the Washington-Baltimore area. One has only to recognize that Harpers Ferry is on a parallel with Baltimore to see the significance of this topography. Conversely, Federals in the Valley threatened *Lee's* strategic flank through New Market Gap as well as the strategic targets of the railroads and access to the Valley's bounty.

Sigel and Grant originally intended the main effort in the Valley to be Crook's and Averell's raids. His force at Martinsburg was to serve as a distraction, with the purpose of luring the Southern defenders away from the raiders. The plan called for a movement south only about as far as Cedar Creek, north of Strasburg. This would seem to threaten Staunton, possibly pulling away its defenders, while still enabling Sigel to protect the eastern half of his department. Sigel altered the plan when he learned that the only force confronting him seemed to be *Brig. Gen. John D. Imboden's* small *Valley*

District Brigade. He decided to move at least as far south as Woodstock. This, he thought, would have a greater chance of pulling Confederate defenders out of southwestern Virginia, and he intended to go on the defensive at Woodstock while sending out strong patrols. Sigel felt the deeper penetration additionally would disrupt Confederate exploitation of the Valley's resources while increasing the threat to *Lee's* strategic flank.

Federal forces began coming into Martinsburg during April from all over northern Virginia, West Virginia, and Maryland. On 1 May Sigel deployed his infantry to Winchester while his cavalry moved even farther south to Strasburg and Cedar Creek. The Federals were to remain in these locations until 9 May. In the meantime *General Imboden* based at Mt. Crawford began to react to the changing threat. He concentrated his forces in the vicinity of Woodstock and on 2 May called out the *Augusta and Rockingham County reserves.* He also sent word of the situation with a request for reinforcements to *General Breckinridge.*

Southern response was prompt and decisive. *General Lee* ordered *Brig. Gen. John H. Morgan's Cavalry Brigade* from Tennessee to Wytheville, thus giving *Breckinridge* a bit more depth. He added *Imboden's forces* and his Valley District to *Breckinridge's* jurisdiction, assuring unity of command. Lee also placed the *VMI Corps of Cadets* at his disposal. *Breckinridge* watched the situation develop and decided that Sigel posed the greatest strategic threat. Therefore, on 6 May he directed *Generals Echols* and *Wharton* to concentrate *their forces* at Staunton; this was achieved by 12 May in a complex logistical operation using road and rail movement and supply coordination. The troops averaged twenty-one miles a day on the march.

While this was going on, *General Imboden* continued to develop the situation. *Captain John H. McNeil* with sixty men staged a spectacular raid on the Piedmont, West Virginia, rail depot on 5 May. The Georges Creek railroad bridge, 7 big machine shops, 9 locomotives, 80 freight cars, and several miles of telegraph lines were destroyed. Another 3 full freight trains were destroyed at Bloomington. The purpose of this devastation was to make Sigel detach some of his strength away from his main body of troops to protect the B & O. As a result, he did leave more troops guarding the railroad than he had planned originally. Further, he became so sensitive to the guerrilla threat that thereafter he deployed substantial portions of his strength to protect his trains.

One of his first reactions was to send Col. Jacob Higgins and 500 men from the 22d Pennsylvania and 15th New York Cavalry Regiments from Winchester to Moorefield to try to capture *McNeil.* Higgins set out on 6 May, the same day *Breckinridge* began to concentrate his forces. *General Imboden* learned of Higgins' expedition, and on 8 May he moved to counter it. Leaving the *62d Virginia Mounted Infantry* in Woodstock, he headed for Moorefield with the *18th and 23d Virginia Cavalries.* The next day, he ambushed Higgins at Lost River Gap near Moorefield and pursued the fleeing Federals north to Old Town, Maryland. When the pursuit ended on 10 May, Higgins' force was no longer a factor.

The same day as Higgins' disaster, Sigel moved his main body from

Winchester to Cedar Creek, establishing his headquarters at Belle Grove Mansion. His approach compounded with bad news for *Breckinridge*. The force under *Brig. Gen. Albert Jenkins* that he had left to confront Crook's advance was defeated at Cloyd's Mountain. *Jenkins* was mortally wounded and captured; however, the fighting had been so severe that Crook was not to follow through on his full objectives. Averell's attack was similarly blunted at Crockett's Cove on 10 May by *John H. Morgan—Breckinridge* could not know this at the time. The situation impelled him late on 10 May to order the *VMI cadets* to join him at Staunton. They set out the next morning, reaching Staunton late on the twelfth, averaging about seventeen miles a day.

Meanwhile, on 11 May Sigel resumed his stately passage up the Valley. He reached Woodstock that night and there learned through telegrams captured at the local office that *Breckinridge* was concentrating his forces against Sigel's at Staunton. This was the first firm intelligence he had received to show that he was facing more than *Imboden's* little force. *Imboden* had returned on 12 May from his triumph against Higgins and had set up defensive positions at Rude's Hill between Mt. Jackson and New Market.

Sigel reacted to a guerrilla raid on his trains at Strasburg that day by sending out another cavalry force. Two hundred men from the 1st New York Cavalry (Lincoln) under Col. William Boyd departed in a driving rainstorm for Front Royal with instructions to screen the Federal eastern flank into the Page Valley, and then to rejoin the force farther south. This detachment is an example of Sigel's pedantic approach to the situation; what Boyd could achieve away from the main body is difficult to perceive. At the same time, his departure reduced Sigel's reconnaissance capability and the size of the force at his immediate disposal.

Sigel's scouts from the 22d Pennsylvania Cavalry brushed against *Imboden's* positions south of Mt. Jackson on the rainy morning of 13 May. While the desultory skirmishing went on, Boyd's column had moved from Front Royal east of the Blue Ridge and reentered the Valley through Thornton's Gap to Luray. It destroyed Confederate supplies in storage there, along with several wagon trains, and headed for the New Market Gap. When the Federal column reached the Gap, troops could be seen moving on the Pike below, heading south through New Market. Colonel Boyd presumed that what he saw was the head of Sigel's column. Against the advice of several officers, he ordered his column forward into the Valley.

Imboden, maintaining his hold on Rude's Hill at 1600, was surprised to see the Federal cavalry coming through the Gap. He sent the *23d Virginia Cavalry* dashing through the town to hold the bridge at Smith's Creek at the base of the Gap. Meanwhile, he led the *18th Virginia Cavalry* farther south, then east to penetrate the Federals' rear. His maneuver succeeded beyond every expectation. The Federals were caught strung out as they tried to cross one of the creek's meanders, and they were decimated. Within minutes, Boyd's force ceased to exist. Twenty-five men were killed, seventy-five were captured, and the remainder became desperate fugitives wandering on Massanutten Mountain. Sigel had lost another substantial part of his force with no visible gains. While *Imboden*

Gabriel C. Wharton (Miller)

was performing so effectively, *Breckinridge* moved his force to Harrisonburg. The next day, 14 May, he came fifteen miles farther north to Lacey's Springs.

Preliminary Moves

In the meantime, *Imboden* was becoming fully engaged. Major Timothy Quinn with 500 cavalrymen mainly from the 1st New York (Lincoln) Cavalry had bivouacked the night of 13 May at Edinburg. Early on the fourteenth, another rainy day, he brought his force through Mt. Jackson and repaired the bridge across the Shenandoah. By noon he had forced skirmishers from the *18th Virginia Cavalry* across Meem's Bottom and over Rude's Hill. The intensity of the fighting increased south of the hill as the defenders launched several charges against the advancing enemy.

Meantime, about 1100 that day, Sigel sent Col. Augustus Moor from Woodstock with the 1st West Virginia and 34th Massachusetts Infantry Regiments and Snow's Maryland Battery. Moor added the 123d Ohio to his impromptu brigade at Edinburg—it had been sent forward earlier to support the cavalry. North of Edinburg, Moor encountered some 900 cavalry under Col. John E. Wynkoop (20th Pennsylvania, 15th New York, 1st New York Lincoln and Veteran, 21st New York and Ewing's West Virginia Battery). He ordered Wynkoop and his command forward to support Quinn. These reinforcements thwarted *Imboden's* charges, forcing him back into New Market by about 1600, and there his artillery halted the Federal advance briefly. At 1700, the Federal infantry came up after nearly seven hours of marching with only one ten-minute break. Its added presence forced *Imboden* to take up positions south of the town as darkness set in.

The first Confederate line was on the high ground west of New Market on a line adjacent to St. Matthew's Lutheran Church along the old River Road

Julius Stahel (MHI)

(now in part *Breckinridge* Street). The growing Federal strength caused *Col. George S. Smith*, commander of the *62d Virginia Mounted Infantry*, to pull his men farther south to Shirley's Hill overlooking the New Market Valley. *Smith* placed *Capt. John McClanahan's Battery (The Staunton Horse)* on the hill and extended a thin line of infantry south of the town east to Smith's Creek.

The Federals established themselves in the town and in the position abandoned by *Smith* to the west. Two guns from Ewing's West Virginia Battery were placed on the extreme west of the line, while Snow's Maryland Battery was based near the Lutheran church. At 2000 Moor ordered the 1st West Virginia Infantry skirmishers to probe *Smith's* positions on Shirley's Hill. They were repulsed vigorously by Confederate pickets and their whole regiment advanced to support them, volleying in the direction of the Confederate positions. A second probe by the Mountaineers was repulsed at 2200, after which things became quiet and all contact was broken as *Imboden* pulled his men farther south. The closest support for Colonel Moor was the 18th Connecticut Regiment, sent to Edinburg from Woodstock by General Sigel earlier in the day. It bivouacked about a mile south of the town, fifteen miles in each direction from the larger Federal elements.

General Imboden had joined *Breckinridge* briefly at Lacey's Springs to explain the situation. *Breckinridge* decided to advance to good defensive positions south of New Market and to entice Sigel to attack him. Accordingly, he had his column moving at 0100 on the rainy morning of 15 May, the *VMI cadets* joining the column at 0130 after spending a gloomy night in the Mt. Tabor Church. The advance began to encounter Federal cavalry vedettes after going about six miles. These caused some delay but, more importantly, alerted Colonel Moor. Moor had his men standing to arms by 0300 and earlier had sent back word to Edinburg for the 18th Connecticut to advance. That unit began a speed march so hastily about 0300 that it left Companies F and H on picket. These were drawn in at daylight and began a forced march without rest or food, running the last two miles. They arrived just in time to go into the battle at the moment of *Breckinridge's* attack.

By about 0600 *Breckinridge's* force had closed to a position just south of the county boundary (the Fairfax line). He held them there in a heavy rain for about two hours while he reconnoitered Colonel Moor's position. Then, after sunrise, he had the *18th Virginia Cavalry* probe Moor's line, hoping this would precipitate a Federal attack on his prepared positions. Disappointed in this, he placed his artillery on Shirley's Hill to continue to harass the Federals and to develop the situation. By then, Colonel Moor had established his line firmly along the old River Road and around the Lutheran church. It continued to be anchored on the west by a section of Ewing's West Virginia horse gunners. East of them the line was filled by the exhausted 18th Connecticut, then the 123d Ohio, and the 1st West Virginia. Snow's Maryland Battery remained in the Lutheran cemetery, and the 34th Massachusetts briefly remained east of the Pike. Additional help was still far to the north. Brigadier General Jeremiah Sullivan left Woodstock at 0500 with the 12th West Virginia, the 54th Pennsylvania, and three batteries (von Kleiser's, Carlin's, and DuPont's). The 28th Ohio and 116th Ohio left Woodstock later at 0800 with the trains, at the same time that Sigel and his staff departed. Sigel could hear gunfire by the time he reached Edinburg, but when he caught up with Sullivan's force at Mt. Jackson he lingered for nearly an hour before continuing farther south.

Meanwhile, *Breckinridge's* and Moor's artillery continued to engage each other. Part of Snow's Battery had moved forward briefly until persuaded of the superiority of the Confederate positions on Shirley's Hill. Major General Julius Stahel, Sigel's cavalry chief, arrived on the scene about 0830 and, while assuming command, took exception to Moor's deployment. Perhaps he was alert to the need to close the gap between Sigel's components. His efforts, however, produced confusion and a growing sense among the troops that they were not being led well. A measure of this confusion may be seen in the experience of the 34th Massachusetts: The regiment was about to breakfast in its position east of the Lutheran church when it was ordered back to the Bushong House. Shortly after arriving, it was marched back to its starting position and ordered to send skirmishers out. No sooner was this accomplished than the unit was pulled back to an assembly area north of the present 54th Pennsylvania monument. Then it was moved westward into its final position on Bushong Hill, having marched about seven miles back and forth for no apparent purpose.

Battle Joined

By 1000 it was evident to *Breckinridge* that the Federals had no intention of attacking him. Consequently, he decided to be the aggressor: "I shall advance on him. We can attack and whip them here, and I'll do it." He ordered his lines forward to Shirley's Hill and maneuvered them around to create the impression of greater strength. Finally, he aligned them so as to appear to be

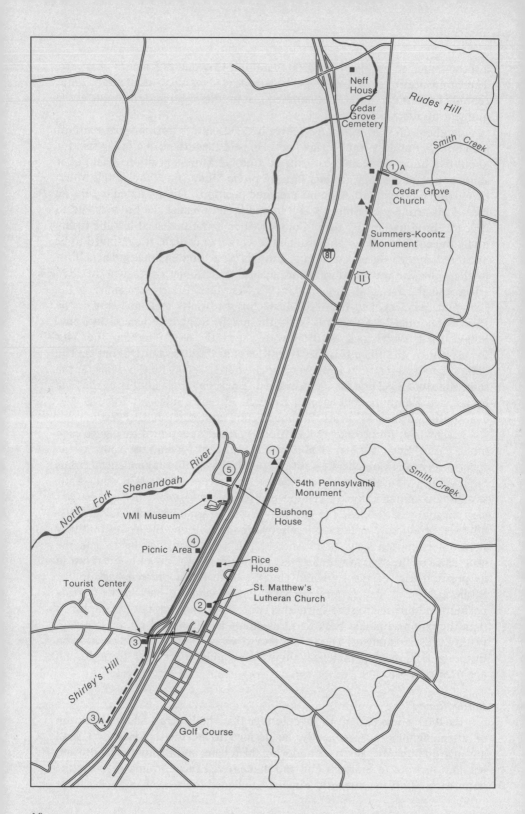

Neff
House

Rudes Hill

Cedar
Grove
Cemetery

Smith Creek

① A

Cedar Grove
Church

81

Summers-Koontz
Monument

II

①

54th Pennsylvania
Monument

⑤

North Fork Shenandoah River

Smith Creek

VMI Museum

Bushong
House

④
Picnic Area

Rice
House

Tourist Center

St. Matthew's
Lutheran Church

②

③

Shirley's Hill

③ A

Golf Course

three strong battle lines, when in reality he had one line staggered in three echelons. *Wharton's Brigade* was in two lines: On the westernmost side was the *51st Virginia*, then the *30th Virginia Battalion* and *Smith's 62d Virginia*. To the right rear of this line was a smaller line composed of the *26th Virginia Battalion* and the *VMI cadets*. *Echols' Brigade* was drawn up farther east by the Pike and south of the village. His *22d Virginia* linked with the troops west of the Pike while the *23d Virginia Battalion* extended east until it connected with *Imboden's cavalry*, which screened the area up to Smith's Creek.

After another hour of bombardment, *Breckinridge's* force began to move forward. The *30th Virginia* preceded *Wharton's Brigade* as it dashed over the crest of Shirley's Hill and down into the New Market Valley. It was followed in the same informal manner by the veteran *51st and 62d Virginia*. But no one had told the inexperienced *cadets* to proceed in open order. Consequently, they marched down the hill with the *26th Battalion* in drill-field formation, providing an excellent target to the fully alerted Federal gunners and sustaining their first five casualties. *Echols' Brigade* pressed forward on the east, conforming to *Wharton's* movement.

The Federal line was set up as described earlier, except that von Kleiser's New York Battery later was to come up to a support position on the Pike a quarter-mile north of the Lutheran church. The 18th Connecticut had dashed up into the line about 1100, just as *Breckinridge's* skirmishers came over the hill. A drenching rain was falling, and the guns continued to duel. Hardtack was issued to the newly arrived troops, but the men could not finish it because of adjustments being made to their line. Companies A and B and, later, Company D of the 18th Connecticut were sent forward from the River Road to the southern brow of the hill to act as skirmishers. While they were doing this, about 1140 *Breckinridge* withdrew his guns off Shirley's Hill and sent them to a position just south of the village. The *cadet gun section* joined them there. Only *Jackson's Battery* remained on the hill to support *Wharton's* advance directly. While this was going on, about 1145 Sigel and Sullivan reached Rude's Hill. Sigel paused briefly to watch the battle, then galloped forward with his retinue. Sullivan remained with his brigade just south of Rude's Hill, awaiting orders.

The Confederate advance resumed about noon. *Breckinridge* had adjusted his line somewhat by bringing the *26th Virginia* up to the west of the *51st Virginia* and sending it down Indian Hollow, a small valley on the west running toward the Shenandoah. This left the *VMI cadets* as his only reserve. On the other flank, *Imboden's cavalry* probed gingerly through woods east of New Market and encountered Federal cavalry facing them. This discovery led *Imboden* to propose going east of Smith's Creek to attempt flanking the Federal position from that side. While he and *Breckinridge* were discussing the plan, Sigel finally arrived in the battle area escorted by Companies F and M of the Lincoln Cavalry. Sigel left his staff at Rice's House and rode forward to the battle line to see things for himself. He quickly decided that there was not time for all his forces in the rear to come forward to Moor's original line; consequently, he directed a withdrawal from the original line back to the high

Infantry Firing Line. (Gilbert Gaul, USMA Museum)

ground on Bushong's Hill. There his flanks would be protected by the Shenandoah's bluffs on the west and Smith's Creek on the east, and he stood a better chance of consolidating his force. Sigel immediately ordered Carlin's Battery to Bushong's Hill and von Kleiser's Battery up to support the withdrawing line. A few minutes later, he directed General Sullivan to bring up the rest of his infantry to the Bushong's Hill position. The literal-minded brigadier complied, leaving DuPont's Battery awaiting orders south of Rude's Hill.

Breckinridge's attack was in full force by this time. The 18th Connecticut skirmishers fell back on the rest of their regiment. The regiment soon extricated itself with some difficulty and fell back with the 123d Ohio to a line about 400 yards farther north, almost on a line with von Kleiser's position on the Pike. About 1230 Sigel ordered Snow's Battery and the 1st West Virginia to withdraw from New Market and to set up on Bushong's Hill, thus vacating the village completely. A half-hour cannonade ensued in the continuing rain. While that was going on, *Imboden* moved the *18th Virginia Cavalry* and one section of *McClanahan's artillery* east of Smith's Creek. *The 23d Virginia Battalion* extended its line to the creek to fill in the gap his departure created. *Imboden* then moved north to a point where his guns could enfilade the Federal flank. This caused General Stahel to pull his cavalry slightly north, behind a ridge just to the north of the present Pennsylvania monument. Ewing's Battery, now back with the cavalry, engaged the Confederate guns to little mutual effect for the remainder of the day. *Imboden* then tried to carry out the second part of his task, which was to destroy the bridge over the Shenandoah at Mt. Jackson to block a Federal retreat. He found the water too high to cross to approach the bridge and rejoined *Breckinridge* at 1600, too late to contribute further to the battle.

The 18th Connecticut and 123d Ohio resisted briefly at their second position, allowing Sigel's final line to form. One of von Kleiser's guns was now disabled on the Pike and had to be abandoned when the battery withdrew. The two infantry regiments were fairly shattered by this time, although Company D of the 18th Connecticut attached itself to the 34th Massachusetts to continue the fight later. *Breckinridge* immediately pressed forward his guns massed on the east as the Federals withdrew. He used his artillery almost as an assault unit in itself, offsetting somewhat his numerical inferiority while helping to suppress some of the fire of the well-handled Federal artillery.

By about 1400, Sigel's final line was almost fully established. On the west overlooking the Shenandoah bluffs, Company C, 34th Massachusetts, provided support to part of a gun line extending along nearly half of the Federal front. Carlin's West Virginia Battery started on the bluff, and to its left was Snow's Maryland Battery, then von Kleiser's Battery of Napoleons. The 34th Massachusetts next took up the line, just about 350 yards due north of the Bushong farm; the 1st West Virginia was to its east. About 1420 the line was extended from the left flank of the 1st West Virginia to the Pike by the 54th Pennsylvania. It had jogged from Rude's Hill after marching from Woodstock with Sullivan earlier in the day. It was preceded on the field by the 12th West Virginia, which placed five companies behind the 34th Massachusetts and its remaining five about 200 yards behind Company C, 34th Massachusetts, on the Federal right flank. About 1430, Captain DuPont brought his battery up the Pike on his own initiative and held it about one quarter mile north of the line while he watched the situation develop.

About that time, the Confederate line had reached the Bushong farm after enduring a growing hail of Federal fire. The *51st* and *30th Virginia* had become somewhat mixed in the advance. The eastern course of the Shenandoah River had squeezed the *26th Virginia* eastward behind the *51st Virginia*. At the same time, the topography on the western side of the *Confederate line* had protected the *26th* and part of the *51st* from much of the fury of the Federal fire. This was not the case for the portion of the *51st* and elements of the *30th* around the Bushong farm. They had reached the farm's northern fence line, but then were forced back to its southern side. The *62d Virginia* on their right had advanced a hundred yards farther before being blasted back with 50 percent losses to a position on line east of the Bushong House. *General Breckinridge* reluctantly directed that the *VMI cadets* fill in the gap left by the *51st Virginia* around the farmhouse. The *cadets* moved on both sides of the house to re-form their line in an orchard, and after climbing over a fence, they lay down and exchanged fire with the Federal line about 300 yards away.

The climax of the battle was fast approaching. General Sigel had noted the discomfiture of the Confederate line and ordered a counterattack, but unfortunately his orders were not clear and they were poorly executed piecemeal. First, about 1445, the Federal cavalry attempted to charge up the Pike. It rode virtually into the mouths of the guns *Breckinridge* had set up on the ridge southeast of the Federal line. The cavalry's position was worsened by the response of the *Confederate infantry*, which briefly faced the Pike on both sides of it, adding a wall of fire on each flank of the quickly decimated Federal horse. The troopers were repulsed with great loss in a matter of minutes. At about this time, a violent thunderstorm was adding to the confusion. Confederate fire continued to build on the Union line. *Jackson's Battery* was deployed southeast of the Bushong House and one company of the *26th Virginia* inched close enough to focus accurate rifle fire on Snow's and Carlin's Federal artillerymen and their teams.

Meanwhile, about 1500 the second part of Sigel's charge was attempted, and each Federal regiment in line lurched forward more or less on its own. The 34th Massachusetts advanced halfway to the Bushong House; however, the 1st West Virginia on its left moved forward barely 100 yards before it gave up. In pulling back, it exposed both the New Englanders and the 54th Pennsylvania on its left, which had gallantly pressed into the Confederates. While this was going on, the fire on the Federal guns became so galling that Sigel authorized their withdrawal. He could see the 28th and 116th Ohio, the train guards, drawing up in line of battle near the Cedar Grove Dunker church two miles north at the base of Rude's Hill, and he directed the guns there. The two Ohio regiments had run the four miles from Mt. Jackson. Snow got away with all his pieces; however, Carlin had to abandon two guns because of the loss of horses, and von Kleiser had to leave a second gun damaged by artillery fire. Carlin lost a third gun because it became irretrievably bogged down during the withdrawal.

This withdrawal of the Federal artillery was marked by a decrease in the volume of fire, and *Breckinridge* sensed his moment had come. A few minutes after 1500 he ordered a general advance. The 34th Massachusetts and 54th Pennsylvania continued to resist valiantly until all the guns that could be were withdrawn. These units then defended rearward until they came under the protection of Captain DuPont's Battery, which delayed skillfully by echelon of platoon back to Rude's Hill. The *Confederate line* swept over the Federal positions, with the *cadets* capturing von Kleiser's abandoned gun along with many men from the 34th Massachusetts. *Breckinridge* removed the *cadets* from the advance about 1520: "Well done Virginians, well done men." Then, impressed by DuPont's opposition and aware of the new Federal line forming at Rude's Hill, he halted his attack about 1600 to reorganize and resupply. The *Confederate artillery*, including the *VMI section*, continued to engage the Federal artillery for another hour.

The Federal main body pulled back across the Shenandoah by 1800, followed an hour later by DuPont and a cavalry escort, which burned the bridge. By the time *Breckinridge* had his victorious force in hand to renew the assault, his enemy had fled. Sigel was so eager to get away that he left his badly wounded in Mt. Jackson and marched the rest of his force through the night and next day until it reached Strasburg the following evening.

Aftermath

New Market unquestionably was what some historians have called the "most important secondary battle of the war." It temporarily unhinged Federal plans for the Valley, preserving its resources longer for the faltering Confederate war effort. Even more significantly, it secured the strategic flank of *Robert E. Lee's forces*, by then seventy-five miles to the east, locked in mortal combat with Grant's and Meade's men. It is not beyond reason to say that the battle extended the life of the Confederacy by nearly a year. This strategic success was one thing; the inspiring example of the *VMI cadets* was another. Theirs was one of several decisive contributions to the battle, the absence of any one of which would have been fatal to Confederate success. However, this group of young men averaging eighteen years of age were not hardened troops. They were called from their campus to fight for a cause in which they believed. They faced reality unflinchingly and gallantly carried out what was expected of them. Their performance had a lasting positive effect on Southern morale and still inspires their successors.

Breckinridge's masterful performance as both a department commander and tactical leader distinguished him as one of the best of many good Confederate generals. Success was possible at New Market because of his prompt assessment of the situation and the flexibility he had incorporated into his defense plans. His innovative tactical measures including the use of deception and the aggressive use of his artillery combined with his strong personal leadership to offset many disadvantages. His success was virtually assured by his willingness to accept the risks necessary for victory. Thus, his disregard of the odds and his gamble to hold nothing in reserve at the critical moment were proved fully justifiable.

Franz Sigel, on the other hand, was the antithesis of this great Southerner. He displayed excessive caution while failing to think through the purpose or value of many of his decisions. He burdened himself with excessively large trains requiring far too much manpower to guard. His disregard for unit integrity led him to send Colonel Moor forward with a mixed collection of units, few of which had worked together before. His lack of organization led to such things as Captain DuPont's being forgotten in the heat of battle while von Kleiser's short-range Napoleons were disadvantageously deployed. Sigel failed to use his staff, personally conducting minor-level reconnaissances and deployments. At the same time, he thought too much of strategy and not enough of tactics, completely ignoring the effect of his decisions on the physical condition of his men. His Chief of Staff, Col. David H. Strother, said of him, "There is no trace of cowardice in Gen. Sigel, as there was certainly none of generalship. Sigel has the air to me of a military pedagogue, given to technical shams and trifles of military art, but narrow minded and totally wanting in practical capacity." Most would agree with Colonel Strother's conclusion, "We can afford to lose such a battle as New Market to get rid of such a mistake as Gen. Sigel."

For a moment New Market made it seem as if another *Stonewall* had come to the Valley. But, although further encouraging moments were experienced in the summer of 1864, the South was inevitably declining. The promise of New Market soon was buried in Federal generalship and numerical and materiel superiority. Thus, by the time of the battle's first anniversary, peace had come to the Valley on Federal terms. The examples of courage and dedication shown in the battle, however, will endure forever.

Suggested Readings

The Battle of New Market has become one of the most chronicled events of the Civil War in Virginia. The role of the VMI cadets has been the particular object of discussion. Any work about the Institute will have a portion devoted to the battle. Articles and letters in the *Confederate Veteran Magazine* are a rich source of anecdotes and comment. Unit histories and personal memoirs also invariably provide a few pages of valuable detail on the fight.

Turner, E. Raymond, *The New Market Campaign, May, 1864*, Richmond: Whittet and Shepperson, 1912. The first scholarly treatment of the battle. Still a sound, balanced work with useful illustrations.

Davis, William C., *The Battle of New Market*, Garden City, N.Y.: Doubleday and Co., Inc., 1975. The only modern book-length study. Rich in detail, the book tends to take a Confederate perspective.

DuPont, Henry A., *The Campaign of 1864 in the Valley of Virginia and the Expedition to Lynchburg*, New York: National American Society, 1925. A broader study that tries to place the battle in relation to the full Valley Campaign as seen by the author, a Federal officer and participant.

Notes on New Market

The first permanent European settlement in the area was made in 1727 or 1728 by Germans from Pennsylvania. A village began to develop at the crossing of the Thornton Gap Road (US 211) and the Old Indian Road (US 11) when John Sevier established a tavern and store there in 1765. The village Sevier started continued to grow, and Sevier went on to distinction as the first governor of Tennessee. The presence of a racetrack was justification for the original name of "Cross Roads" being changed to "New Market" after a British town of the same name famous for its racetrack. One of the first publishing firms west of the Blue Ridge was formed here in 1806, existing until recent times. While prospering commercially from its location on the Valley Pike (US 11), chartered in 1834, the town also became known for its educational institutions.

In 1859 sectional tensions led to the founding of the town's own militia unit, the New Market Cavalry. This unit was mustered into Confederate service as Capt. W.H. Rice's Battery. It became part of the Second Corps, Army of Northern Virginia. The unit saw service in Jackson's 1862 Valley Campaign and all of the later campaigns in Virginia leading to Appomattox. A second local unit, the Emerald Guards, became Company E, 33d Virginia Infantry, part of the Stonewall Brigade. One of the 33d's commanders, Col. John F. Neff, came from Rude's Hill north of New Market. Killed at Second Manassas, he is buried at Cedar Grove Cemetery, where Sigel's men rallied after the battle, 15 May 1864. Confederate troops moved in force through the town three times in Jackson's campaign of 1862. The town also was visited in 1862 by the Federals, Maj. Gen. Nathaniel Banks using the Rice House (Stanley Hall) as his headquarters. The town saw further Federal occupation in June 1864 when Hunter's force moved south to Piedmont and Lynchburg. During their brief stay, the Federals reburied their casualties from the May battle. That fall, the surrounding farms were victims of Sheridan's "burning." After the Battle of Cedar Creek, 19 October 1864, Jubal Early's forces regrouped at New Market for three weeks before probing north one final time. Major Confederate forces left the village for the last time in December 1864 when Early moved farther south into winter quarters around Waynesboro and Staunton. Ten thousand Federal cavalry, under Custer and Merritt, passed through the town in late February 1865, en route to the final battles in Virginia.

The village was the site of the earliest Memorial Day in the South, 15 May 1866.

Chronology

1864	EVENT

Feb   John C. Breckinridge is appointed to command C.S. Department of Western Virginia.

Mar   U. S. Grant develops strategic scheme to exert pressure and mass at all points.

10 Mar   Maj. Gen. Franz Sigel is appointed to command U.S. Department of West Virginia.

30 Apr   Federals under Sigel advance south from Martinsburg.

5 May   Capt. John H. McNeil conducts raid on B & O shops at Piedmont and Bloomington.

6 May   Col. Jacob Higgins and 500 men from 22d Pennsylvania and 15th New York Cavalries leave Winchester for Moorefield.

9 May   Sigel departs Winchester.

9 May   Crook defeats Jenkins at Battle of Cloyd's Mountain.

*9 May   Higgins' cavalry column is ambushed by Imboden (18th and 23d Virginia Cavalries) at Lost River Gap near Moorefield, is chased to Romney and eventually Springfield, West Virginia. (Sixty-mile rout ends night of 10 May.)

10 May   VMI cadets are alerted late at night.

Sigel camps north of Cedar Creek.

11 May   VMI cadets (264, including 7 cadre) begin march north, 0700 reach Midway, 18 miles.

11 May   Echols' and Wharton's brigades concentrate at Staunton.

11 May   Sigel continues south 0700, reaches Woodstock 1600; there Confederate telegram messages are captured and Sigel learns of Breckinridge's presence.

12 May   Cadets arrive at Staunton.

12 May   Imboden sets up line north of New Market.

*13 May   Col. William Boyd with 200 men from 1st New York (Lincoln) Cavalry arrives at New Market Gap; crosses Smith Creek at 1700. Is attacked and dispersed by Imboden (18th and 23d Virginia Cavalries).

13 May   1600: Breckinridge leaves Staunton.

14 May   0500: Breckinridge leaves Harrisonburg (18 miles from Staunton).

1900: Breckinridge reaches Lacey's Springs, 15 miles.

Col. Augustus Moor leaves Woodstock with 1st West Virginia, 34th Massachusetts, 123d Ohio Infantries, Snow's Maryland plus one-half of Ewing's G 1st West Virginia Batteries and cavalry under Col. John E. Wynkoop, Wynkoop's 20th Pennsylvania (170 men), 15th New York (130 men), 1st New York (Lincoln), 1st New York (Veteran), 21st New York Cavalry (600 men) (c. 2,350 men of all arms).

1500: Moor becomes engaged at Mt. Jackson.

1800: He pushes Imboden through New Market, sets up on New Market Valley.

Sigel sends 18th Connecticut to Edinburg.

2000: Col. G. S. Smith defends with artillery from Shirley's Hill; he had a thin line from there to the Smith Creek Bridge.

Federal position is on Bushong's Hill south to New Market Valley, east to Smith's Creek.

15 May   0100: Breckinridge leaves Lacey's Springs for New Market, 7 miles.

0130: VMI cadets move out from bivouac at Mt. Tabor Church, Lacey's Springs.

0300: Col. Moor has all his units on line.

---

* These two engagements eliminated one-third of Sigel's cavalry strength.

0500: Confederates arrive at point about 4 miles south.

15 May 0700: Col. Moor learns of the presence of Breckinridge's troops and sends 34th Massachusetts back to Bushong's, then recalls.

0800–1000: Artillery duel, Imboden's cavalry makes feints to draw out Moor.

1000: Breckinridge decides to attack.

1000–1100: Confederates deploy on Shirley's Hill and move about to give impression of greater numbers.

c. 1100: 18th Connecticut, less three companies, arrives from Edinburg (15 miles) and immediately deploys.

(The first Federal line was on the brow of Manor's Hill.)

c. 1100: Confederates begin attack preceded by 30th Virginia as skirmishers.

c. 1140: Confederate artillery deploys from Shirley's Hill to just south of New Market on both sides of the Pike. Jackson's Battery remains with infantry.

c. 1200: Attack begins through ankle-deep mud.

26th Virginia is brought on line on extreme west to go down Indian Hollow. There was little Federal resistance except from the 18th Connecticut opposite the 51st Virginia.

1200: Sigel arrives on the battlefield.

1230: New Market is completely cleared of Federals; one-half hour cannonade ensues.

c. 1300: Imboden with 18th and 23d Virginia Cavalries and four guns crosses Smith's Creek to flank Stahel.

c. 1345: Confederates renew attack in driving rainstorm—mud and knee-high grain.

Confederate artillery sets up on north edge of town.

c. 1415: Sigel's main line is set up.

(Sullivan leaves Woodstock 0500, arrives at Mt. Jackson c. 1030 with 28th Ohio (—), 116th Ohio, and DuPont's Battery.)

15 May c. 1420: 54th Pennsylvania comes into line after a forced march from bivouac at Mt. Jackson; it had left Woodstock that morning. It followed the 12th West Virginia onto the battlefield.

1430: Dupont's Battery arrives south of Rude's Hill.

1440: Part of 51st Virginia and 30th Virginia north of Bushong's north fence are pounded by Federal artillery and begin to waver and pull back to fence; Woodson's men engage in sharpshooting Kleiser's.

1445: Confederate line is stalled everywhere.

Breckinridge directs commitment of VMI cadets.

The cadets move through the Bushong property to the north fence. The 26th Virginia fills in rest of gap.

1445: Federal cavalry charges down the Pike, into artillery with 22d Virginia on west and 23d Virginia on east flanks, are easily repulsed amid violent thunder and lightning. 12th West Virginia moves up behind guns and 34th Massachusetts.

One company of the 26th Virginia approaches Federal batteries on the river bluff.

1500: Sigel orders charge by infantry on west (34th Massachusetts, 1st West Virginia, 54th Pennsylvania).

1st West Virginia moves 100 yards, is halted by Confederate fire and falls back. This exposes the 54th Pennsylvania to encirclement in its charge, forcing its withdrawal.

34th Massachusetts on other side of 1st West Virginia advances even farther, loses 200 men, and retires.

1505: Confederate west line charges. 34th Massachusetts continues firing to give artillery time to withdraw (54th Pennsylvania continues resistance [254 casualties out of 566], the highest of any unit engaged.)

Snow's Battery withdraws first with all guns.

Carlin is forced to abandon three pieces during withdrawal.

1520: Breckinridge orders the cadets

out of pursuit. "Well done Virginians, well done men."

15 May 1530: Federal line forms on Rude's Hill, 116th and 28th Ohio anchor line west from Cedar Grove Dunker church. DuPont delays by platoon.

1600: Confederates pause for an hour to reorganize and resupply.

Artillery duel continues, including VMI section.

c. 1730: Federals continue withdrawal.

c. 1900: DuPont burns Shenandoah Bridge.

2100: Federals retire from Mt. Jackson to Cedar Creek.

16 May Sigel retreats to Cedar Creek.

17 May Breckinridge's force is entrained for Lee's army.

19 May Sigel is relieved and given local command at Harpers Ferry.

21 May David Hunter takes command of Federals at Cedar Creek.

26 May Hunter begins advance south.

5 Jun Hunter defeats W. E. Jones at Battle of Piedmont.

17 Jun Early's Corps begins to arrive in Lynchburg; Breckinridge places himself under Early's command.

18 Jun Hunter is defeated at Battle of Lynchburg.

27 Jun Early reorganizes and moves down Valley.

3–4 Jul Early's forces bypass Harpers Ferry garrison, cross Potomac at Shepherdstown.

8 Jul Early reaches Frederick, Maryland; sends Johnson's Cavalry Brigade to raid Baltimore and Point Pleasant Prison.

9 Jul Early defeats Lew Wallace at Battle of Monocacy.

11 Jul Early reaches Silver Spring, Maryland; VI Corps arrives and occupies Washington defenses; 1st Div., XIX Corps, en route to Petersburg from New Orleans, is diverted from there to District of Columbia.

12 Jul Skirmishing at Ft. Stevens, Washington, D.C.; Early makes a night withdrawal.

14 Jul Early crosses Potomac at White's Ferry, near Leesburg, Virginia.

18 Jul General Horatio Wright establishes contact with Early at Snicker's Gap; is joined by Crook of Hunter's command. Battle of Cool Spring.

20 Jul Federal cavalry under W. W. Averell defeats Ramseur at Stephenson's Depot.

22 Jul Federals enter Winchester.

22–23 Jul Early defeats Crook at Second Battle of Kernstown; advances and wrecks Martinsburg rail yards; then chases Crook to Williamsport, Maryland, by 26 July.

29 Jul VI Corps returns to Harpers Ferry after learning of Kernstown.

30 Jul Confederate cavalry (John McCausland and Bradley T. Johnson) burns Chambersburg, Pennsylvania. Early's northern thrust causes almost as great a stir as his District of Columbia raid. Grant decides to defeat him and/or make the Valley unusable to him.

5 Aug Grant visits Hunter at Monocacy. Federals occupy Halltown positions south of Harpers Ferry. Early sends troops across Potomac at Williamsport and at Shepherdstown, gathering a harvest (diversion to help his cavalry in Pennsylvania).

7 Aug Federal Middle Military Division is created under Philip Sheridan to coordinate against Early. [Included VI Corps (Wright), VIII Corps (Crook), XIX Corps (Emory), and Cavalry Corps (Torbert).] Month of maneuvering follows. McCausland and Johnson are routed at Moorefield, West Virginia, by Averell.

3 Sep Meeting engagement at Berryville between Crook and Kershaw. Kershaw's recall is deferred.

4–15 Sep Skirmishes north and east of Winchester.

14 Sep Kershaw's division departs for Lee's army.

19 Sep Sheridan defeats Early at Third Battle of Winchester or Opequon; Early retreats to Fisher's Hill.

20 Sep Sheridan follows to Strasburg, Vir-

ginia. Pickets on opposite sides of the villages.

21 Sep   Breckinridge is ordered back to Department of West Virginia.

22 Sep   Early is defeated at Battle of Fisher's Hill and is pursued eventually to Harrisonburg; Sheridan begins "burning" as far south as Staunton, Virginia. Federal cavalry is reorganized, with Merritt and Custer given divisions. Kershaw and Rosser, in the vicinity of Culpeper, are ordered back to support Early.

23 Sep   VI and XIX Corps advance from Woodstock, VIII Corps polices battlefield. Early pulls back from Narrow Passage to Mt. Jackson, then is pushed back to Rude's Hill by Federal cavalry.

24 Sep   VI and XIX Corps, in Mt. Jackson, are joined by VIII Corps. Battle line presses Early south. Brief skirmish occurs in New Market.

25 Sep   Early continues south to Port Republic, is joined by Kershaw's Division on 27 September. Sheridan arrives at Harrisonburg.

28 Sep   Early moves to Rockfish Gap; retreat ends.

1 Oct   Early takes up position at Mt. Sidney, midway between Staunton and Harrisonburg. Feeling it logistically impossible to proceed farther, Sheridan decides to pull north.

5 Oct   Grant initially agrees to withdrawal and Sheridan burns his way north, but Grant reconsiders the move.

6 Oct   Sheridan departs Harrisonburg and camps at Rude's Hill that evening.

7 Oct   Early's main force reaches New Market.

8 Oct   Sheridan arrives at Strasburg. Rosser presses Federal cavalry hard; Merritt holds at Tom's Brook; Sheridan commands Torbert to turn and fight, "either whip the enemy or get whipped yourself."

9 Oct   Battle of Tom's Brook. Sheridan watches from Round Hill. The fight lasts two hours, Lomax is pursued to Mt. Jackson, Rosser to Columbia Furnace.

10 Oct   Sheridan camps north of Cedar Creek; turns down a plan to open Manassas Gap Railroad.

13 Oct   Early closes forward to Fisher's Hill; he sends a force to Hupp's Hill and engages Thoburn's Division with artillery (Stickley's Farm). Wells' and Harris' Brigades deploy across Cedar Creek; Kershaw's Division deploys off Hupp's Hill. Harris' Brigade is forced back and Wells is enfiladed by James Connor's Brigade. Meanwhile, Confederate cavalry on the Back Road attacks Custer.

19 Oct   Sheridan defeats Early at Battle of Cedar Creek.

20 Oct   Early retires to New Market. Stays there three weeks, cavalry at Edinburg, reinforcements from south West Virginia.

26 Oct   Federal cavalry probe is repulsed at Milford in Fort Valley.

9 Nov   Sheridan pulls back to Kernstown.

10 Nov   Early moves to Woodstock.

11 Nov   Skirmish takes place at Middletown.

12 Nov   In cavalry skirmish at Cedarville, Confederates are defeated.

22 Nov   In skirmish at Rude's Hill, Federals are repulsed.

6–16 Dec   Early's reduced forces go into winter camps in the vicinity of Staunton and Waynesboro; Gordon's Corps is recalled to Richmond.

1865

27 Feb   Sheridan proceeds south from Winchester.

2 Mar   Remnants of Early's force are annihilated at Waynesboro by Custer. Sheridan goes on to join Grant.

VMI Cadets

In 1839 the Virginia legislature approved replacing the guard company at the Lexington Arsenal with a military school. The school was intended to provide a source of competent militia officers, engineers, and teachers. It proved to be the state's greatest source of officers in 1861; of sixty-four regiments raised that year, twenty-two were commanded by VMI graduates. Of 1,902 VMI matriculates from 1839 to 1865, 1,781 served in the Confederate Army. In April 1861 the Corps of Cadets, 200 strong, performed training duties in Richmond. The school resumed "normal" operations in January 1862 with 269 cadets. The corps was called out as reserve in April and May 1862 during Jackson's McDowell Campaign and took to the field three times in 1863 to support resistance against Federal cavalry raids in southwest Virginia. Following New Market, the corps was ordered to Richmond, where it served briefly in the city's defenses. It returned to Lexington in June to resist Hunter's advance, but could do little to prevent the Federal burning of Institute facilities. The corps was furloughed from July to October, when it was reassembled at Richmond where it served again periodically in the city defenses. It was disbanded on 2 April 1865 on the eve of the evacuation of Richmond. The Institute reopened at Lexington in October 1865.

VMI Casualties

Killed in Action:
  Cabell, William H.
  Crockett, Charles G.
  Jones, Henry J.
  McDowell, William H.
  Stanard, Jaqueline B.
Died of Wounds:
  Atwill, Samuel A., 20 Jul 64
  Hartsfield, Alva C., 26 Jun 64
  Haynes, Luther C., c. 15 Jun 64
  Jefferson, Thomas G., 18 May 64
  Wheelwright, Joseph C., 2 Jun 64
Wounded in Action:
  Akers, Reuben C.
  Berkeley, Edmund, Jr.
  Bradford, John F.
  Buster, William D.*
  Christian, Edward D.
  Cocke, John P.
  Corling, Charles T.

Darden, James D.
Dickinsen, Jesse I.
Dillard, William, Jr.
Garnett, Griffin T.
Garrow, Harris W.
Gibson, Franklin G.
Goodwin, James H.
Harris, Willis O.
Harrison, Carter H.
Hill, Archibald G.
Howard, John C.
Imboden, Jacob P.
Johnson, Porter
Jones, Walter S.
Macon, George K.
Marshall, Martin
Mead, Henry J.
Merritt, James L.
Moorman, Edwin S.
Pendleton, Robert A.
Phillips, Samuel T.
Pizzini, Andrew, Jr.
Preston, James B.

---

* Died of typhoid April 1865 with corps at Richmond.

Randolph, Charles C.
Read, Charles H.**
Shipp, Scott
Shriver, Samuel S.
Smith, Charles H.
Smith, Edward H.
Smith, Francis L.
Spiller, George
Stuart, John A.
Triplett, John R.

Upshur, John N.
Walker, Charles D.
Walter, Charles P.
Watson, William P.
White, Thomas W.
Whitehead, Henry C.
Wise, John S.
Wise, Louis C.
Woodlief, Pierre W., Jr.
Wyatt, John W.

VMI Cadets at New Market. (B. W. Clinedienst, courtesy of VMI)

Order of Battle

Both the forces engaged were provisional, assembled from scattered forces operating for the most part on security and antiguerrilla missions. The Federals had been gathered from numerous isolated posts over the six weeks preceding the battle. Few of the units had performed before in standard brigade and division operations. General Sigel had completed assembling his forces at Martinsburg and Winchester on 29 April. He developed his organizational structure during his slow movement south. Even more immediately, the Confederate forces were gathered as the Federal plan revealed itself. General Breckinridge began to consolidate his forces on 7 May, completing his new arrangement at Staunton on 12 May, three days before the battle.

Order of Battle
New Market, Virginia, 15 May 1864
U.S. Department of West
Virginia—Maj. Gen. Franz Sigel

First Infantry Division—Brig. Gen. Jeremiah C. Sullivan
1st Brigade—Col. Augustus Moor
18th Connecticut Infantry—Maj. Henry Peale
28th Ohio Infantry—Lt. Col. Gottfried Becker
116th Ohio Infantry—Col. James Washburn
123d Ohio Infantry—Maj. Horace Kellogg
2d Brigade—Col. Joseph Thoburn
1st West Virginia Infantry—Lt. Col. Jacob Weddle
12th West Virginia Infantry—Col. William B. Curtis
34th Massachusetts Infantry—Col. George D. Wells
54th Pennsylvania Infantry—Col. Jacob M. Campbell

First Cavalry Division—Maj. Gen. Julius Stahel
1st Brigade—Col. William B. Tibbitts
1st New York Cavalry (-) (Veteran)—Col. Robert F. Taylor
1st New York Cavalry (Lincoln)—Lt. Col. Alonzo W. Adams
1st Maryland Cavalry (det.) (Potomac Home)—Maj. J. T. Daniel
21st West Virginia Cavalry—Maj. Charles C. Otis
14th Pennsylvania Cavalry—Capt. Ashbel F. Duncan
2d Brigade—Col. John E. Wynkoop
15th New York Cavalry—Maj. H. Roessler
20th Pennsylvania Cavalry—Maj. R. B. Douglas
22d Pennsylvania Cavalry (det.)—1st Lt. Caleb McNulty

Artillery
Battery B, Maryland Light (3" rifle)—Capt. Alonzo Snow
30th Battery, New York (12-lb. Nap.)—Capt. Albert von Kleiser
Battery D, 1st West Virginia Light (3" rifle)—Capt. John Carlin
Battery G, 1st West Virginia Light (3" rifle)—Capt. Chatham T. Ewing
Battery B, 5th United States (3" rifle)—Capt. Henry A. DuPont

C.S. Western Department of Virginia
—Maj. Gen. John C. Breckinridge

Infantry Division
1st Brigade—Brig. Gen. John Echols
22d Virginia Infantry—Col. George S. Patton
23d Virginia Battalion—Lt. Col. Clarence Derrick
26th Virginia Battalion—Lt. Col. George M. Edgar
2d Brigade—Brig. Gen. Gabriel C. Wharton
30th Virginia Battalion—Lt. Col. J. Lyle Clark
51st Virginia Infantry—Lt. Col. John P. Wolfe
62d Virginia Infantry (Mtd.)—Col. George H. Smith
Co. A, 1st Missouri Cavalry (Inf.)—Capt. Charles H. Woodson

23d Virginia Cavalry (Inf.)—Col. Robert
White
VMI Cadets—Lt. Col. Scott Shipp
Cavalry, Valley District—Brig. Gen. John D.
Imboden
18th Virginia Cavalry—Col. George W.
Imboden
Misc. dets. 2d Maryland, 23d Virginia, 43d
Virginia (Partisans)
Artillery—Maj. William McLaughlin
Chapman's (Virginia) Battery (4 how., 2
rifle)—Capt. George B. Chapman
Jackson's (Virginia) Battery (1 rifle, 3 12-lb.
Nap.)—1st Lt. Randolph H. Blain
McClanahan's (Virginia) Battery (2 how., 4
rifle)—Capt. John McClanahan
VMI Section (2 rifle)—Cadet Capt. C. H.
Minge

Total Effectives

Federal Forces

Infantry	5,245	(approx. 3,750 engaged)
Cavalry	3,035	(approx. 2,000 engaged)
Artillery (22 guns)	660	(approx. 530 engaged)
Total:	8,940	(6,280)

Confederate Forces

Infantry and dis- mounted cavalry	4,249	(approx. 3,800 engaged)
Cavalry	735	(all engaged)
Artillery (18 guns)	341	(all engaged)
Total:	5,325	(4,876)

Casualties

Federal: 97 KIA, 520 WIA, 225 MIA
= 841 (13%)
Confederate: 43+ KIA, 474+ WIA, 3 MIA
= 531+ (c 13%)

Notes on Ordnance

Three-Inch Ordnance Rifle
- Fires 10-lb. projectiles (conical bolt, case, shell, canister)
- Bore diameter, 3 "
- Tube weight, 820 lbs., wrought iron
- Range, 1,830 yds. at 5° elevation
- Muzzle velocity, 1215 FPS
- Use: Infantry support in open areas, counterbattery.

12-Pound Field Gun, M1857 (Napoleon)
- Fires 12-lb. projectiles (solid, case, shell, canister)
- Bore diameter, 4.62"
- Tube weight, 1227 lbs., bronze
- Range, 1,619 yds. at 5° elevation
- Muzzle velocity, 1485 FPS
- Use: Close infantry support in wooded areas, final defense.

Parrot Field Rifle, 10-pounder
- Fires 10-lb. projectiles (conical bolt, case, shell, canister)
- Bore diameter, 3 "
- Tube weight, 890 lbs., iron
- Range, 2,000 yds. at 5° elevation
- Muzzle velocity, 1300 FPS
- Use: Same as ordnance rifle.

Field Howitzer, 12-pounder
- Fires 12-lb. projectiles (solid, case, shell, canister)
- Bore diameter, 4.62"
- Tube weight, 788 lbs., bronze
- Range, 1,072 yds. at 5° elevation
- Muzzle velocity, 1200 FPS
- Use: High-trajectory antipersonnel.

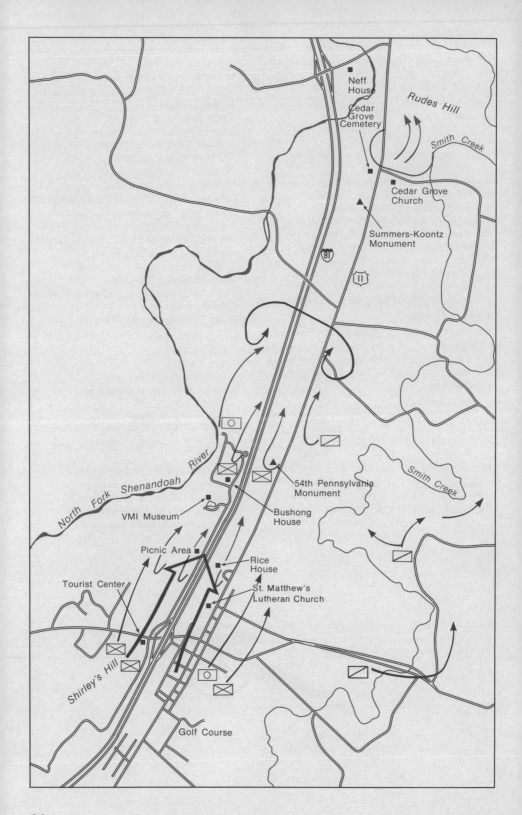

Neff
House

Cedar
Grove
Cemetery

Rudes Hill

Smith Creek

Cedar Grove
Church

Summers-Koontz
Monument

North Fork Shenandoah River

Smith Creek

54th Pennsylvania
Monument

VMI Museum

Bushong
House

Picnic Area

Rice
House

Tourist Center

St. Matthew's
Lutheran Church

Shirley's Hill

Golf Course

New Market is located along Interstate 81 about 55 miles south of Winchester and 80 miles north of Lexington. Take exit 67 (New Market) and either begin your tour as described below or visit the Virginia Military Institute Hall of Valor. This may be reached by turning right off the exit, then making an immediate right onto the Collins Parkway (CR 619). Proceed two miles north on the Parkway and you will see the Hall of Valor on your left (west).

The 54th Pennsylvania Memorial was dedicated by members of the regimental association on 25 October 1905. It was funded jointly by the association and the Keystone State and placed on a small plot donated for the purpose. Title to the land was transferred from Pennsylvania to the Battlefield Park in ceremonies on 19 September 1984.

Pennsylvania Monument

Begin your tour at the 54th Pennsylvania Monument on US 11. This is located 1.5 miles north of the center of New Market. It may be reached from exit 67 off Interstate 81 by going .4 mile east to New Market on CR 260 and 1.5 miles north on US 11. The monument is on the west side of the road. Park and walk to the monument.

The monument marks the eastern limit of the final infantry line established by General Sigel about noon on 15 May. The Pennsylvania troops trotted into the location about 1420, less than 40 minutes before the decisive Confederate charge. They first occupied the low ground north of the monument, then charged south approximately 200 yards toward the tree line before being forced back. A few minutes before their charge, the Federal cavalry had attempted to advance. However, as it galloped across a small stone bridge to the east of the Pennsylvanians (70 yards northeast of the monument) it came under devastating artillery fire compounded by rifle fire from both sides of the Pike as it progressed. It was repulsed with considerable loss in a matter of minutes.

This position is about half a mile west northwest of the position occupied by McClanahan's gun section set up by General Imboden east of Smith's Creek. Fire from those pieces caused the Federal cavalry originally located to the southwest to pull back to the ground north of the monument and east of the Pike. From there, it later launched its ill-fated charge.

Boyd's cavalry was decimated about .9 mile east of here on 13 May after emerging from New Market Gap. Captain James H. Stevensen of the New York Lincoln Cavalry described the fight.

As we descended the mountains we discovered a large body of troops marching up the

Valley Pike, from Mt. Jackson towards New Market, and we sent word to Colonel Boyd who came galloping to the front.

The colonel thought [they were friendly] and ordered us to advance. In a short time we saw a section of artillery and some cavalry moving rapidly toward the base of the mountain, at a point some distance south of where we must strike the valley. . . . Colonel Boyd . . . seemed a little staggered, but concluded to proceed, observing that they must be Sigel's troops. On reaching the base of the mountains, we found some pickets at a little bridge on Smith's creek, but they were dressed in our uniform, and Colonel Boyd thought they were some of Sigel's men who had not been informed of our approach.

They retired on our advancing towards them without attempting to fire. I sent a few men to push them, and they set off at full speed for New Market. We then held a little "pow-wow," and it was determined to cross the bridge, pass down the stream and try to gain the turnpike in rear of the column of troops which we had seen marching toward New Market. Then, if they were the enemy, we could show them our heels and bid them defiance. We crossed the bridge, and were just in the act of crossing the stream, which makes a bend across the little valley, when the bluff above us, on the New Market side, became alive with horsemen. The next instant we heard the well-known "rebel yell," accompanied with a shower of bullets and shouts of "Now we've got the d _____ d Yankees! give 'em h _____ l!"

The firing was so hot from the bluff, and a shell bursting over us at that moment, the men under Boyd gave way, notwithstanding his example of courage and coolness.

Rude's Hill and Return

A digression from the main tour can give a useful sense of the dimensions of the northern part of the battlefield and of key sites. Should you wish to do this, continue north 3 miles to CR 616. Turn right, go .1 mile to the Cedar Grove Church. Built in 1857, this was the structure noted by Sigel from Bushong's Hill, around which the 28th and 116th Ohio regiments were forming. By 1600 on 15 May they had set up a line of battle just north of the church on the slope of Rude's Hill. Sigel directed his forces on Bushong's Hill to rally on the church.

Return .1 mile to US 11 and the Cedar Grove Cemetery.

The Federal units fleeing Bushong's Hill rallied in this area before withdrawing farther north. DuPont's Battery set up on the south side of the cemetery after its masterful withdrawal and engaged Confederate guns a mile away, which were located in an orchard now marked approximately by CR 767 crossing over Interstate 81.

The cemetery contains the graves of many notable local persons including those of Col. John F. Neff, who commanded the 33d Virginia Infantry of the Stonewall Brigade before being killed at Second Manassas. His house is the brick building .8 mile northwest by road down US 11, then west on CR 730 to just west of the Shenandoah on the way to Interchange 68 of Interstate 81. Instead of turning on CR 730, if you go north another .1 mile from the junction with US 11, on the west side of the road you will see the Rude House and farm. Built before 1792, this was used as a headquarters by Stonewall Jackson in April 1862

Cedar Grove Dunker Church, 1920. (Wayland)

and by the Federal David Hunter in June 1864. In October 1864, Capt. John H. McNeil was mortally wounded in a cavalry fight on Meem's Bottom, which stretches to the north. He was brought to the house where later he was interviewed by General Sheridan. Sheridan recognized McNeil's condition and left him alone. The dying Confederate later was removed to Harrisonburg where he expired. Meem's Bottom saw considerable cavalry fighting throughout the war. In April 1862, Jackson's men camped in the area. Later, Federal Brig. Gen. James Shields deployed his entire division across the Bottom as he maneuvered against Jackson's rear guard. In the course of Shields' advance, Turner Ashby's white charger, "Tom Telegraph," was mortally wounded while Ashby tried to destroy the bridge. The gallant animal managed to carry his master out of danger up the Pike to a mile below New Market before collapsing. The Bottom was a camp site for Jubal Early's Division in November 1863. Early used "Mt. Airy" on Smith's Creek to the east for his headquarters. The approximately 1,500 men captured at Waynesboro camped on the Bottom under guard on 6–8 March 1865 waiting for the water levels to drop sufficiently to be able to ford the Shenandoah. While they were here, the remnants of Rosser's cavalry attacked Federal positions on Rude's Hill in a vain attempt to liberate the prisoners.

Return from CR 730 3.6 miles to the 54th Pennsylvania Monument. En route about .1 mile south of the cemetery, notice the stone marker in the field.

This is a memorial to Cap. George W. Summers and Sgt. Newton Koontz of Page County. They were shot on 27 June 1865 on this spot by order of a Lieutenant Colonel Huzzy of Ohio. The men had come over on business and did not

29

have the necessary parole documentation. Their execution was an unwarranted atrocity.

Continue toward the Pennsylvania monument; as you drive south, you will pass the positions taken by DuPont's two gun platoons late on 15 May. The second position occupied by 2d Lt. Charles Holman's section was on the west side of US 11 opposite the point where CR 732 joins US 11. The position occupied by 2d Lt.

Benjamin Nash's section is .3 mile farther south, east of the Pike opposite the large chicken house. Another .2 mile south marks Sgt. Samuel Southworth's position east of the Pike just south of the modern farm lane. Finally, Lieutenant Holman's first position is .18 mile closer to the monument on the west side of the Pike, about where the modern restaurant is located. **Continue the remaining .375 mile back to the monument.**

St. Matthew's Lutheran Church

From the 54th Pennsylvania Monument, drive south on US 11 1.5 miles to the parking lot of St. Matthew's Lutheran Church. In .4 mile you will come to two motels. These motels mark the final Confederate artillery positions. Breckin-

54th Pennsylvania Monument, 1987. (© J.W.A. Whitehorne)

ridge deployed his guns on the ridge east of the Pike that extends northeast toward Smith's Creek. Ten guns under the command of Maj. William McLaughlin, including the two-gun cadet section, brought heavy fire on the Federal line and were instrumental in stopping the Union cavalry charge. **Continue .3 mile to a point opposite the closed Battlefield Gift Shop. A modern natural wood house is west of US 11.** This marks the point about where Captain von Kleiser's New York gunners first set up to support Colonel Moor's forward line. The position also marks the eastern side of the intermediate line occupied by the 18th Connecticut and 123d Ohio after they pulled north from the River Road. One of von Kleiser's guns was disabled here, its wheel knocked off by Confederate fire, and had to be abandoned. **Continue .1 mile to the Shenandoah Retirement Home.** This was the home of Capt. W. H. Rice who raised the Shenandoah-Page Battery, which he commanded until losing a leg at Cross Keys in June 1862. The house was built by his father, Dr. John Rice, in 1834. The building also

Rice's Barn, 1920. (Wayland)

was used as a headquarters by General Shields during the 1862 campaign. A barn stood until 1926 north of the house where the white townhouses are now. It was one of the main hospitals after the battle. **Continue .3 mile to St. Matthew's Lutheran Church, turn west, .1 mile into the church parking lot, and stop.** The Federal dead from the battle were buried hastily in a field along US 11 between the church and Rice's House, because the local citizens did not want them in consecrated ground. They were later reinterred more substantially by Federals in June, then removed to Staunton after the war.

Snow's Maryland Battery set up in the cemetery area late on 14 May. Early on 15 May, Captain Snow sent a section forward to about where the fast food restaurant is located east of the Interstate 66 Interchange. This position was so dominated by Breckinridge's artillery on Shirley's Hill that the Federal gunners pulled back to their positions by the church. The 34th Massachusetts was in line to the east of this location on the other side of US 11 until it began its odyssey. Later, Major McLaughlin's guns moved up to a position in the vicinity of the present school a bit farther east. West of the parking lot a small lane may be seen heading towards the interstate. This is the last vestige of River Road, another trace of which can be found west of the interstate. The 1st West Virginia set up along this road from about the west side of the parking lot to a point midway to the interstate. The 123d Ohio extended the line to just past the interstate. Ewing's West Virginia Battery set up on the high ground. It was later joined, early on 15 May, by the 18th Connecticut, which formed line westward from the 123d Ohio. The Federals were completely driven from this entire line by 1230 on 15 May.

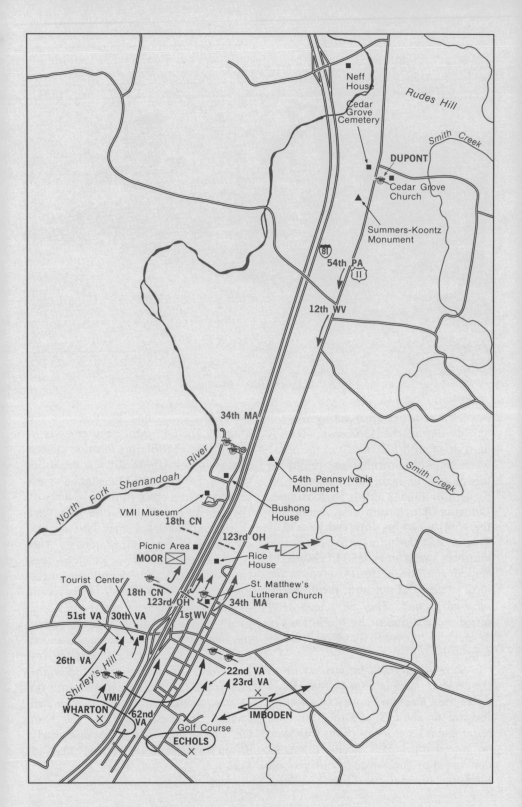

Neff House

Rudes Hill

Cedar Grove Cemetery

DUPONT

Smith Creek

Cedar Grove Church

Summers-Koontz Monument

54th PA

12th WV

Smith Creek

34th MA

54th Pennsylvania Monument

North Fork Shenandoah River

VMI Museum

Bushong House

18th CN

123rd OH

Picnic Area

MOOR

Rice House

18th CN

123rd OH

St. Matthew's Lutheran Church

Tourist Center

34th MA

51st VA   30th VA

1st WV

26th VA

Shirley's Hill

22nd VA

23rd VA

VMI

WHARTON

62nd VA

IMBODEN

Golf Course

ECHOLS

An obelisk in the middle of the cemetery marks the Confederate burial ground. Also, at the entrance to the church area, by US 11, is a post containing a conical bolt fired by a Federal battery. Allegedly, Breckinridge and his staff clustered on US 11 were the targets of this shot. No harm was done other than scattering the group with splinters. The house on the opposite side of the lane was built in 1790 and was the home of Confederate veteran George M. Neese, author of the memoir *Three Years in the Confederate Horse Artillery*.

Drive from here to the Shenandoah Valley Tourist Association Building west of Interchange 67.

New Market Valley ③

From St. Matthew's Lutheran Church, drive .3 mile to the traffic light at CR 260 (Old Cross Roads). En route, one block south of the church on the east at the corner of US 11 and Seminary Road is a building which was occupied by the Federal provost marshal during Reconstruction. At the crossroads, notice the large building on the southeast corner. This was the Lee-Jackson Hotel, the home of Dr. Joseph B. Strayer at the time of the battle. Stonewall Jackson reviewed his men from this corner in May 1862 as they turned east, bound for the New Market Gap. In the fall of 1864, the building was used as a headquarters by Maj. Gen. Jubal Early. **Turn west onto CR 270 and proceed .4 mile under the Interstate and turn left (south) into the parking lot of the Shenandoah Valley Tourist Association. (You are back by Interchange 67.)** This is the New Market Valley referred to earlier. South of the parking lot is Shirley's Hill over which Wharton's Brigade came, while to the north is Manor Hill on which the 18th Connecticut skirmishers deployed. Northwestward is some low ground bounded by Manor Hill and another hill with some houses on it. This is Indian Hollow down which Lt. Col. George M.

Edgar's 26th Virginia Battalion advanced.

The 30th and 51st Virginia dashed over the brow of Shirley's Hill and down into this area. As they pressed forward, Edgar's Battalion and the VMI cadets then marched over Shirley's Hill in formation, offering a target for the Federal artillery. The first five VMI casualties were sustained on the northern slope of the hill. When they got to the bottom into the little valley, they grounded their packs along the road and watched the first wave press the Federals north, then followed in reserve.

Lieutenant Colonel Scott Shipp, Commandant of Cadets, described the situation.

As Wharton's line ascended a knoll it came in full view of the enemy's batteries, which opened a heavy fire, but not having gotten the range, did but little damage. By the time the second line reached the same ground the Yankee gunners had gotten the exact range, and their fire began to tell on our line with fearful accuracy. It was here that Captain Hill and others fell. Great gaps were made through the ranks, but the cadet, true to his discipline, would close in to the center to fill the interval and push steadily forward. The alignment of the battalion under this terrible fire which strewed the ground with killed and wounded for more than a mile on open

33

View of Shirley's Hill from St. Matthew's Lutheran Church. (Turner)

View of Battlefield, looking north from Shirley's Hill, 1888. (courtesy of Coiner Rosen)

ground, would have been creditable even on a field day.

The cadets held briefly along CR 260 and prepared to advance. Captain Frank Preston observed,

Marching down the first hill we were exposed to the enemy's batteries, but were too far to reply with arms. In this advance one man was killed in the first line, and several wounded in our Battalion. . . . After getting to the bottom of the hill we were entirely covered, and here we waited half an hour, while some change was made in the lines. A half hour of intense suspense—the artillery on either side firing—the shot and shell flying and bursting high over our heads—knowing that in a short time we must charge the infantry, whose dark lines we saw drawn up in the woods. . . . After some time the first line began to move forward up the hill. . . . Then the second line began to move, and our nerves were strung and our lips firmly closed, our breath coming short and quick, waiting for the crash of musketry which we expected would receive the first line.

The cadets eventually headed north in support of the battle, as described by Cadet John C. Howard.

We now marched on down the hill in front, which was a right steep one. There was a road at the bottom, and just beyond the road a fence. Crossing this fence we were halted and ordered to take off blankets and everything else except gun and equipment. This looked like business, stripping for the fight, and we began to think our work was really cut out for us. "Attention, Battalion! Forward!" This was the beginning of that long-ascending field, the main theater of the fight. The ascent at first was steeper than it afterwards became, but in a very little while we were within range of the Federal infantry as well as artillery as they directed their fire against the line. I heard the hiss of the bullets and saw where they had struck the ground in different directions, right, left, and in front, but I was a green hand, and didn't know that this meant we were among the Minie balls. A few minutes after being under fire we were halted, and the corps commenced marking time; but as we lay down almost instantly for a few seconds, a cadet near me remarked:

"What damn fool gave the order to mark time under this fire." We were up again almost instantly, and then forward. We could clearly hear the firing of the Southern artillery over our heads, and hoped it would silence some of the hostile guns in front —which, in a measure, it did.

Williamson's Hill

It is possible if you are in a private automobile to drive to the final assembly areas of Wharton's Brigade, occupied before the attack. **Turn south from the Tourist Association parking lot and drive .8 mile along CR 619, which parallels the Interstate. Go to the first dirt driveway on your left, just before the white frame house. Make a "U" turn in the driveway and halt on the side of the road. The driveway is a private road; do not block it, and be alert to traffic as you turn. Your route has taken you along one side of Shirley's Hill and behind it.**

The Confederates left US 11 about a half mile southeast of this point and marched to the southern base of Shirley's Hill. The 30th Virginia Battalion and 51st Virginia advanced north onto the slope of the hill and moved around to give the impression of greater strength. The cadets took up a position along the fence line extending east from the driveway where you turned. The 26th Virginia Battalion took up the line farther east, out onto the flats extending to the Pike, where it linked with Echol's Brigade.

Col. George S. Smith, 62d Virginia (New Market Battlefield Park)

Breckinridge came up to this part of the line and encouraged the cadets, as recalled by Cadet Howard.

We were ascending the slope of the long hill with the ridge in view, and our next stopping place was after crossing a fence several hundred yards below this ridge and out of the range of all hostile fire. At this point the Confederate lines began their advance. . . . When the cadet battalion reached this position by the fence, it was put in to fill a space, and became then part of the second line of battle, halting with the other troops while they watched the advance of the first line of battle over the ridge in front. Just at this point, General Breckinridge, in command of the Southern troops, rode up with his staff and halted near. He was greeted with something of a cheer, and said to the battalion of cadets: "Young gentlemen, I hope there will be no occasion to use you, but if there is, I trust you will do your duty." The instant thought in my mind was: "What do you mean by that? Here we are, a part of the second line, and if it advances, we will have to advance with it." My thoughts, however, had nothing to do with the situation, and I was engaged, like the rest, in watching the advance on the first line of battle, some hundreds of yards away, that was moving over the high crest of the hill. We had heard in some way that the range from point to point of artillery had been obtained by the Federals all along where they thought the battle was likely to be fought. This was probably true. At any rate it was true as to that particular hill, and we saw the bursting of a number of shells as the first line passed over. I think there was but little damage done by this fire.

Return .8 mile to the Tourist Association.

Picnic Area

Turn north from the Tourist Association parking lot, proceed across CR 270, past the cannon, and go .68 mile to the second entrance of the picnic area. Once across CR 270, you are on the Collins Parkway, which leads eventually to the VMI Museum.

When you reach the crest of Manor Hill, .2 mile from CR 270, notice the buildings on the west. The 18th Connecticut skirmishers set up along here forward of the empty restaurant building. As quoted from Maj. Henry Peale, 18th Connecticut,

We here awaited the approach of the enemy, whose skirmishers in double line could be seen issuing from the woods covering his position. The artillery duel still continued with considerable vigor, and the enemy shelled our line with great accuracy, although without inflicting any considerable damage. Companies A & B were immediately deployed, and descended the hill. Severe skirmishing shortly ensued.

The enemy in three strong lines, now issued from the woods and charged down the hill at double quick, his skirmishers also increasing their step and driving ours more rapidly.

It was at this time decided that a small knoll, some 200 yards to the rear, would afford a better position, especially for the artillery, which could inflict greater damage upon the enemy who would be forced to pass over an eighth of a mile of nearly level ground before reaching our lines. The line accordingly marched in retreat.

And as Maj. R. F. Lang, 1st West Virginia, recalled,

In the center just on the left of the Valley turnpike through my strong field glasses I beheld an unfamiliar sight for the battlefield, a body of several hundred with bright uniforms, shining swords, . . . polished buttons, and handsome flags . . . kept the alignment perfect . . . on came the line, and on came the bright uniforms.

Another .3 mile will take you to the vestiges of River Road that have survived west of the interstate. Notice that you are on a parallel with St. Matthew's Lutheran Church, whose spire you can see to the east. This marks the western part of Colonel Moor's line and was held by the remainder of the 18th Connecticut. Ewing's guns were about 100 yards west down River Road. In his official report Major Peale stated,

The new position of the regiment was most unfortunate . . . being in a lane backed by barns and two rows of fence. A continuous rain of 5 days had rendered traveling on other than the roads extremely difficult, and the men stood knee deep in mud. As the lane was entered by the flank, so nothing but a flank movement could extricate the regiment in order. Companies A & B [skirmishing forward] were now strengthened by Company D, leaving only 4 companies in line, in all somewhat less than 200 men.

The skirmishers of the enemy now appeared

on the brow of the hill and rapid firing ensued. . . . As our skirmishers retired around our flank, the line fired several volleys, when it became apparent that the line of the enemy greatly outnumbered our own . . . the order to retreat . . . was followed [starting on left brigade]. The regiment, marching by the flank at a double quick, on emerging from the lane found itself some distance in rear of the retreating line and was thereby thrown into some confusion, but with some exceptions the men were rallied, and were reformed.

And as Adjutant E. B. Culver, 18th Connecticut, wrote,

It was no wonder there was some confusion in the retreat, the ground being in horrible condition; the mud so deep from previous rains that it was almost impossible to keep in line when no hasty movement was required. And to add to the confusion the rain began to pour again in torrents, greatly retarding the progress.

A final .2 mile brings you to the picnic grounds maintained by the VMI Museum. Pull in here and park. Looking east, you have a good view of the New Market Gap, Rice House, and the school that marks the area of McLaughlin's next-to-last artillery position. A few yards south, in the other part of the picnic area, the cadets sustained two more casualties, while another two were incurred about 50 yards to the northwest of where you are. The area was swept by intense federal artillery fire. According to Cadet Howard,

Fifty yards or so to our right was a Confederate officer who had been wounded and was lying nearly prostrate on the ground. Not quite, however; he was resting on his left elbow, and, forgetful of self, apparently oblivious of his wounds, his handsome young face shone brightly and his sword waved from side to side in sympathetic encouragement of his comrades. Another shell exploded and he was cut down for the second time. Prostrate now, and with the "Last Roll Call" sounding in his ears, the heroic soul still waved [his sword] back and forth under the self-renunciatory impulse of the life leaving the earth and to its acclaim in heaven. If it may be so vouchsafed, I pray that I may meet this knight of the bloody plain there on the bloodless plain hereafter, amid the vales of verdure and glades of ever-flowing green, and let him gather from my face how he has been borne for more than half a century in the breast of one, at least, in cherishing, revering admiration.

What effect that waving sword may have had as a cheering incentive on anyone else—for many beside myself must have witnessed the incident—I do not know, but I know there was no giving back as we pressed forward through the storm.

Battlefield Park

Drive north from the picnic area .5 mile to the gate to New Market Battlefield Park. En route, at .2 mile, notice the unpainted outbuilding and the nearby green mileage marker on the east side of the interstate. These are on a line with von Kleiser's first position, which you visited earlier. The 18th Connecticut and 123d Ohio briefly formed a line along this area and delayed the Confederate advance. First Lieutenant Charles M. Keyes recorded,

. . . slowly we began to retire—taking our cannon back through a cedar thicket, our pathway marked with the blood of our braves. As they appeared over the eminence we had lately occupied, they poured in upon us such a storm of shot and shell, so thick that the very air seemed alive with bullets. On passing through here on our way up the valley a month later, we examined this spot, and found scarce a tree or bush unmarked, showing that the fire at this point must have been severe indeed.

On the crest of the hill beyond another stand was made, which checked their advance for a short time, but soon we were again compelled to fall back, this time pretty badly shattered. Major Kellogg, commanding the regiment, had his horse shot from under him and received quite a severe wound himself. He, however, was supplied with another horse by the officer commanding a battery near at hand, and again rallying his command,

which fell back in good order.

Continue .3 mile to the museum gate. You can turn west .2 mile to the museum and visit that now, or continue .15 mile straight ahead to the white Bushong House and visit the museum at the end of your tour. Park in the space available adjacent to the Bushong House.

The next part of the tour will consist

David H. Strother (MHI)

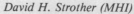

Bushong House, 1911. (Turner)

of a 1.2-mile walk around the final battle area. Before starting this, a tour of the Bushong House and its grounds would be of interest.

Bushong House. The Bushong family migrated in 1731 from Switzerland to Pennsylvania and were established in the New Market area by about 1810. The main house, open to visitors today, was built about 1825. The family endured the engagement in the house, taking refuge in the ground floor kitchen, and after the battle both house and barn were temporary hospitals. The family's kindness toward Federal wounded led to their outbuildings' being spared during the later Federal "burning." Acquired by VMI alumnus George R. Collins in 1944, the property was bequeathed to the Virginia Military Institute in 1964 to become the nucleus of the battlefield park.

Jackson's Battery, 62d Va.

From the Bushong House parking lot, walk about 60 yards southeast to a point between the blacksmith shop and Interstate 81. About 30 yards south of you, note the single gun. It denotes the approximate final location of Jackson's Battery, which followed in direct support of the advancing Confederate infantry. General Breckinridge observed events around the Bushong House from a point several hundred yards to the southwest, closer to US 11.

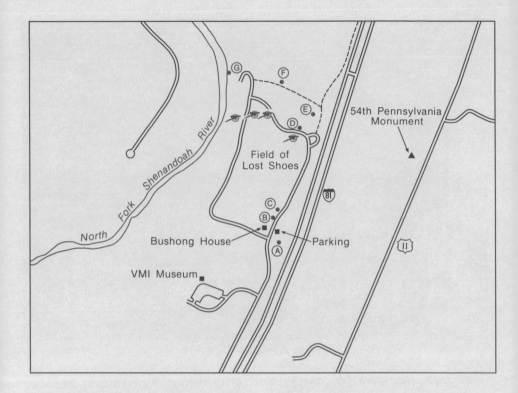

Looking directly north you will see a shallow gully beginning near the Bushong House parking lot. It is intercepted by the interstate but continues eastward about 250 yards toward US 11. Colonel George S. Smith's 62d Virginia, with Captain Charles H. Woodson's Co. A, 1st Missouri Cavalry attached, moved through the gully to the ridge about 200 yards to the north. There, the regiment hit a wall of Federal artillery and infantry fire and fell back to the relative shelter offered by the gully. Colonel George H. Smith, 62d Virginia Mounted Infantry, recalled,

When we reached the line of the fence beyond Bushong's house, the right of the 51st Regiment became exposed to a heavy fire from the enemy's line, and the regiment halted and commenced firing. The 62d continued to advance, and on passing the slight elevation in front of it and reaching the depression beyond came under the close concentrated artillery and infantry fire of the Federal line, losing in a very few minutes over two hundred of the men. The whole loss of the regiment in the fight was two hundred and forty-one out of an aggregate of about five hundred, including seven of the captains. These, it should be mentioned, were eleven in all, including Captain [Woodson], commanding a company of Missourians, which had been temporarily assigned to us, which did good service and suffered severely. Seeing it impossible to effect anything with the remaining two hundred and fifty or two hundred and sixty men, I ordered the regiment to fall back, which it did, halting after passing the elevation referred to and immediately re-forming and upon the 22d Regiment coming on its left, and advancing with it.

Cpt. Conrad Currence, G. Co., 62d Va., was killed trying to grab his colors. Of the 11 companies making up the regiment, seven lost their commanders. 100 out of 442 men were lost in this ravine. The fire was the hottest I was ever under.

Farther west, the 30th and 51st Vir-

Ground Crossed by 62d Virginia. (Turner)

ginia were having an equally bad time. The men had forged their way forward against the Federal fire through the Bushong property to a fence on its north side. The intense fire proved too much for many of them and they began to drift back to the greater shelter offered on the south side of the Bushong buildings. General Breckinridge noticed this and ordered his aide, Maj. Charles Semple, to go over and restore order. Semple pointed to the cadets standing in reserve in what is now the open field between the museum building and the Bushong House and asked, "General, why don't you put the cadets in line? They will fight as well as our men?" Breckinridge replied, "No, Charley, this will not do, they are only children and I cannot expose them to such a fire as our center will receive." Semple ran over and found the situation irretrievable. He came back to Breckinridge and said, "General, it is too late. The Federals are right on us. If the cadets are ordered up we can close the gap in our center." Breckinridge then ordered: "Major, order them up and God forgive me for the order." Cadet John H. Upshur described the VMI Corps' movement forward.

On the northern border of this field and to our front, stood Bushong's house, beyond which was an apple orchard. The enemy had slowly fallen back and taken up a third position several hundred yards beyond this house. On reaching the house, the ranks divided, A and B Companies passing to the right of the house, and C and D Companies to the left; A and B marking time until the other half came up and the line was reformed.

Cadet Willis O. Harris recalled in a 1909 letter to Cadet Capt. Henry A. Wise,

In passing over the ground occupied by the farm-house . . . and its outhouses and orchard, we were thrown into disorder, especially in getting over a picket fence.

41

Bushong's Orchard

Bushong Orchard, 1911. (Turner)

Walk one hundred yards from near the blacksmith shop back through the parking lot north on the road until you are about halfway past the orchard. The experience in the orchard was described vividly by Cadet Howard.

We were halted in an inclosure surrounding a dwelling, and ordered to lie down just in front of the house. It would have been more satisfactory to my inner feelings had we been behind the house. I look back upon that orchard as the most awful spot on the battle field, and, as the shot and shell tore over and around us, I was reminded by their malignant shriek of the driving snowstorm, whose flakes I could see, and marveled not at the number hit, but that all were not killed. Lying next to me was Edward B. Smith, who was struck by a spent ball, though we did not know at the time it was spent. I heard it strike—the hip, I believe—and the sound was as if some one had struck an empty cask with a hammer. I was glad that no contemporary laden messenger treated me in similar fashion. Ross—next to my other side—spoke to Smith, asking if he were wounded. But there was no time for more than the affirmative reply when an order came to move. A crisis had been reached: the fire was too hot for irresponsive action, and retreat or advance was the alternative. We considered a retreat no part of the game, and "forward" was the order. We were halted for some reason before climbing the fence of the inclosure. I saw a cedar tree a yard high or thereabout, with a trunk as big as my thumb. Not a very effective defensive, but, no matter, anything from a white oak to a wheat straw was better than nothing, and I threw myself down behind it. One of the company, Ashleigh, apparently concluded that if a tree of that dimension could protect one person it might perhaps be stretched to protect two, and threw himself down full length on my body. A bullet tried to find us, but fortunately failed, cutting the trousers of both without touching the leg of either. Ashleigh escaped also the rest of the day. In the darkening light I gave him a drink from my canteen, and told him of Randolph's wound. I remember the emotion his countenance expressed. Randolph, whose wound we then thought fatal, was very generally popular in the Corps, and he and Ashleigh had been intimates. And now once more forward. The first thing to do was climb the fence, which impressed itself on me so indelibly as never to have been forgotten. It was an ordinary rail fence, probably about four feet high but as I surmounted the topmost rail I felt at least ten feet up in the air and the special object of hostile aim. But in clearing this obstruction I was leaving all thought of individuality behind.

Woodson's Monument

Continue north about 20 yards until you are on the north side of the tree shading the small monument. The modest Missouri monument was built in May 1905 by two former members of Woodson's command, at their own expense. You are standing on the final line held by the Confederates preparatory to their successful charge. Once over the orchard fence, the cadets lay down for about fifteen minutes, and for the first time in their long advance they were able to return the Federal fire. The rain and smoke by this time made visibility difficult. Colonel J. H. Waddell, 12th West Virginia, described what could be seen from the Federal side.

At a given order they fell flat on the ground, and we could see nothing but a gray streak across that meadow. Directly they arose on their knees, and immediately a streak of fire and smoke flashed across that field, and the bullets flew thick and fast through our ranks.

The Federal line was stretched from east to west about 350 yards to the north of this position. The guns on the hill to the northwest symbolize the batteries of Snow and Carlin. The single piece by the lone tree marks the location of von Kleiser's Battery. The seventeen pieces Sigel arrayed on the slope extended from the top of the hill at least down to the single gun. Directly in front of this point and extending east to the interstate is the part of the line occupied by the 34th Massachusetts. It approached to within about 100 yards of this spot in its unsuccessful charge.

Its repulse marked the start of the Confederate assault. Lieutenant Colonel Scott Shipp described the fortunes of the corps during this period.

The advance was thus continued until having passed Bushong's house, a mile or more beyond New Market, and still to the left of the main road the enemy's batteries, at 250 or 300 yards, opened upon us with canister and case-shot, and their long lines of infantry were put into action at the same time. The fire was withering. It seemed impossible that any living creature could escape; and here we sustained our heaviest loss, a great many being wounded and numbers knocked down, stunned, and temporarily disabled. I was here disabled for a time, and the command devolved upon Captain H. A. Wise, Company A. He gallantly passed toward. We had before this gotten into the front line.

Continue north from this point about 320 yards to the end of the lane. En route, notice the deep basin in the field west of the road. This area was planted in knee-high wheat at the time of the battle and the ground was totally saturated by the extended rains. The muddy surface restricted the men to a slow walk and sucked their footwear off as they struggled forward, hence the name for the area: "Field of Lost Shoes." As described by Capt. Frank Preston in the Lexington *Gazette,* 25 May 1864,

The mud, which in many places was over the ankles, made it impossible to advance faster than at a walk, and the enemy's artillery had fair range all the while.

Cadet Wyndham Kemp recalled in a letter to Brig. Gen. James M. Goggin,

We had to cross a ploughed field where the mud was up to our ankles. Here I remember that one of my shoes pulled off in the mud, and I went through the rest of the "row" with nothing on one foot but a sock, and I'm prepared to "Make affidavit" that there wasn't much of that.

Again, in the *Gazette*, Captain Preston recalled,

In the advance of this third position, we were subjected to a terrible fire of artillery. When within four hundred yards of their line three of our boys fell dead from the explosion of one shell—Cabell, Jones, and Crockett, and fifty yards further on McDowell, from my company, fell pierced through the heart with a bullet.

Cadet Gideon Davenport later recounted to Capt. Preston Cocke,

The bursting of shells about us was incessant,

Sigel's Hill and Field of Lost Shoes, looking north from Bushong's Orchard, 1911. (Turner)

one of these passing directly through our colors. . . . About this time we passed a group of wounded soldiers who cheered us, but a shell, intended for us, burst in their midst, and they were silent. Suddenly there was a crash in our front—a great gap appeared in our ranks, and 1st Sergeant W. H. Cabell, privates Wheelwright, Crockett, and Jones fell dead, and others were wounded. The opening was immediately closed, and the line went forward in the best of order. Nothing could have been finer done.

Cadet Kemp continued to General Goggin,

I remember here a circumstance that we, the Cadets, thought nothing of, believing it unusual under like conditions, but which some of the old soldiers, who saw it, afterwards applauded. In advancing under heavy fire of shells and shot over the uneven and muddy ground, the wings of our battalion pushed forward, making our line crescent-shaped. In order to correct this our commandant gave the order he was used to give us on the parade-ground at drill, that is to "mark time"; and this we did under fire, until the command "forward" was given.

Von Kleiser's Position, 34th Massachusetts

Continue walking the 320 yards to the end of the lane and parking area. Pause inside the split-rail fence on the gravel path leading toward the artillery pieces. You are slightly forward of the western flank position of the 34th Massachusetts Infantry. The regiment took position in the slight hollow just to the north of this point. Von Kleiser's five guns were in position close to where the single piece stands today. Colonel George D. Wells and Lt. Col. William S. Lincoln, the 34th Massachusetts commander and second in command, described the regiment's experience in this area, according to Lincoln,

While the regiment was awaiting the advance of the enemy, the men of Moore's [sic] line came back "on the double quick, some of them running through and over our lines."

The advance of the Rebels, before which Moore's line had given way, was steady and continued. The air was filled with bullets and bursting shells; but, as yet, we had sustained no harm. Colonel Wells took his position at the left, sending Lieut. Colonel Lincoln up to the right of the Regiment. Now Company G, Capt. Leach, was detached, and sent forward as skirmishers to cover our front. "It went

forward, deploying about 200 yards in advance, with a precision and steadiness never surpassed on drill"; but, upon reaching the crest of the hill, was recalled, and, passing through our lines, formed in rear of their proper place in regimental line. Spent bullets were falling thickly among and around us, but inflicting no injury. Now, from some unexplained cause, the 12th Virginia opened fire, over the heads of our men, causing the first casualties of the day; and it was only by the most active efforts of Gen. Sigel, and our own Lieutenant Colonel, who rode among their lines to aid their own officers, that the seeming demoralization of this command was checked, and order restored.

And as Colonel Wells stated in the *Official Records of the Union and Confederate Armies,*

The officers, in the line, were giving their orders in low tones; and every man stood, his gun at the ready, his finger on the trigger, waiting to see the face of his foe. It was a marvel to me then, and is now, how men, who almost never before had heard the Rebel yell, and the terrible din of the battlefield, could be so entirely calm and self-possessed. Soon, our men in front were, by the confusion, cleared away, the Rebel lines were plainly seen, and the battle began. Our front fire was heavy; and the Artillery had an

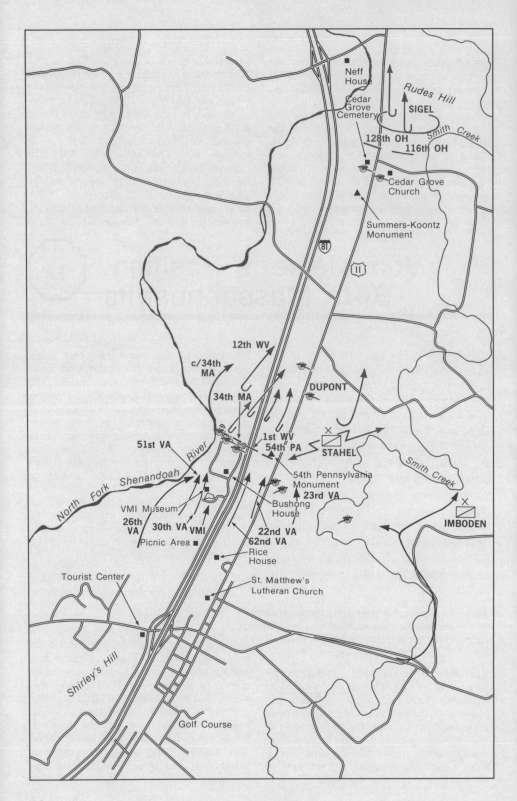

Neff
House

Cedar
Grove
Cemetery

Rudes Hill

SIGEL

Smith Creek

128th OH

116th OH

Cedar Grove
Church

Summers-Koontz
Monument

81

II

12th WV

c/34th
MA

34th MA

DUPONT

51st VA

River

1st WV
54th PA

STAHEL

Shenandoah

North Fork

54th Pennsylvania
Monument

23rd VA

Smith Creek

VMI Museum

26th
VA   30th VA **VMI**

Bushong
House

22nd VA
62nd VA

IMBODEN

Picnic Area ■

Rice
House

Tourist Center

St. Matthew's
Lutheran Church

Shirley's Hill

Golf Course

Col. George W. Wells, 34th Massachusetts Infantry (Miller)

enfilading fire, under which their first line went down. They staggered, went back, and their whole advance halted. Their fire ceased to be effective. A cheer run along our line, and the first success was ours. I gave the order to "cease firing."

In a letter to the Reverend Mr. James H. Smith, 10 March 1888, published in the Richmond *State*, Lincoln remembered,

I well recollect even now our own position, the field of battle, and the appearance of each army. We were upon the right of the infantry line; to our right, upon ground slightly elevated, a six-gun battery. The Sixty-second Virginia, which formed the extreme left of the attacking force, advanced directly against us. To the right of the Sixty-second were the cadets. The line of advance was a little diagonal to that of our formation, and as it was continued the Sixty-second passed beyond and the cadets came directly to our front. Our fire, both that of artillery and infantry, was rapid and continuous, and, when the battery opened with canister, was destructive. As the advance was continued, it was apparent that the cadets were in advance of the general line of the attacking force. Here their forward movement ceased, and for

a moment it seemed as if their advance was checked. But what seemed a check was in reality a halt, during which "those boys" marked time, dressed their ranks, and when again aligned on the left, came forward in most admirable form. The whole thing was done with as much precision and steadiness as if on parade, and this while all the time subjected to a destructive fire. No one who saw it will ever forget it. No command but one most admirably drilled and disciplined could have done it.

The two Bay State officers further recalled the Federal charge and withdrawal. Said Wells,

Just then, Colonel Thoburn, Brigade Commander, rode along the lines, telling the men to "prepare to charge." He rode by me, shouting some order I could not catch, and went to the regiment on my left, which immediately charged. I supposed this to be his order to me, and commanded to fix bayonets, and charge. The men fairly sprang forward. As we neared the crest of the hill, the regiment on my left, which first met the fire, turned and went back, leaving the 34th rushing alone into the enemy's line. I shouted to them to halt, but could not make a single man hear or heed me; and it was not until they had climbed an intervening fence, and were rushing ahead on the other side, that I was able to run along the lines, and, seizing the color bearer by the shoulder, hold him fast, as the only way of stopping the regiment. The wings surged ahead, but losing sight of the colors, halted. The alignment rectified, we faced about, and marched back to our position, in common time.

And to continue, Colonel Lincoln rendered in his account of the battle,

A charge of the whole line was now ordered. Our men sprang forward with a cheer. Our dogs, of whom we had a small army, ran frolicking and barking before us, as they had so often done, on drill. Receiving the fire of both lines, they were nearly all killed. Here, at the very front of our advance, fell Lieut. R. W. Walker, of A, as was then supposed, mortally wounded. We poured a rapid and well directed fire into the enemy; which, aided by the heavy enfilading fire from our artillery, checked his advance. For a moment

47

he staggered, appeared to give way, and the day seemed ours. The rain was falling in torrents; and this, with the smoke, which settled down thick upon us, hid the field from observation. Gallant as was our own charge, the order had met with feeble response on our left, where the troops, turning, went back, suffering little loss, and inflicting less upon the enemy. While Breckinridge was moving his main force against our front . . . opened his artillery within point blank range. Exposed to this flank fire, the 54th Pennsylvania, after a short but stout resistance, was led from the field by its brave commander, upon his own responsibility.

An order to retreat came up to us from the left. We fell back slowly, and in good order; the men, as well as the officers, crying out, "Steady! Keep your line! Don't run, 34th!" It was impossible to see to any considerable distance, so thick was the smoke and rain. Suddenly, [Cpt] Bacon's voice was heard, calling upon his men to stand by the colors; and in response to what was supposed to be a general movement of the line, the right companies were halted, faced about, and became again warmly engaged. A determined charge upon our front, and a withering fire poured into our left flank, and rear; from the now contracting lines of the Rebels, was too much. The Color Company turned; its gallant Captain received his death wound, and the companies of the right wing followed their comrades to the left in retreat. Just at this moment our Lieutenant Colonel [Lincoln] fell, severely hit by shot, and shell, and, unable to continue in retreat, was left in the hands of the enemy. Our troops kept on in slow and sullen retreat till they reached Rhude's [sic] Hill.

Federal Line

Walk about 30 yards from the von Kleiser/34th Massachusetts position to the graveled service road where it leaves the parking lot and passes through a gate in the fence into the pasture. Notice the 54th monument due east across the interstate highway. Colonel Jacob M. Campbell, commander of the Pennsylvanians, reported on his regiment's charge as the battle climaxed.

. . . my regiment . . . took position on the left of the First West Virginia and in the extreme left of the line of battle. We remained in this position, partly shielded from the fire of the enemy by the crest of a hill in front until, observing the regiment on my right making a charge in the absence of orders, presuming it proper to imitate their example, I ordered the Fifty-fourth also to charge, which was done with alacrity and spirit. Advancing beyond the crest of the hill, a rapid, vigorous, and, as I believe, effective fire was for some time kept up on the enemy, and every effort made by them to advance on the front occupied by my regiment was firmly and resolutely resisted and proved abortive, although we sustained a galling and destructive fire, in which many of my men were killed and wounded. The enemy, however, pressed forward his right, which extended some distance beyond our left, and was rapidly flanking me in that direction despite the most determined resistance, when my attention was called to the fact that the regiment on my right . . . had given away, and the enemy advancing at almost right angle with my line and extending beyond the rear and right of my regiment. A few minutes only would be required to completely surround my regiment, and in the absence of any appearance of advancing support I was reluctantly compelled to order my command to retire. This was done in as good order as the circumstances would allow, two stands being made by a portion of the command before passing beyond musket-range, and the whole of it finally rallying and forming at a point indicated by the Colonel commanding the brigade.

Walk 50 yards north along the service

road until you reach a hedge line. This was the location of five companies from the 1st West Virginia. The 34th Massachusetts with the 1st West Virginia were pushed back through this area, and Col. George D. Wells recalled,

. . . The Rebel line advanced, until I could see, above the smoke, the battle flags on the hill where the artillery had been posted. I ordered a retreat, but they either could not hear or would not heed the order. I was finally obliged to take hold of the color bearer, face him about, and tell him to follow me, in order to get the regiment off the field. They fell back slowly, firing in retreat, and encouraging each other not to run.

But the Rebels were coming on at the double quick, and concentrating their whole fire upon us. I told the men to run, and get out of fire as quickly as possible, and rally behind the first cavalry line found to the rear. The colors were halted several times, by different officers, in positions where it was impossible to make a stand, and would only start again at my direct order. I felt much relieved on receiving an order from Gen. Sullivan, who was conspicuous on the field, that the line would be formed on the ridge, and no stand made before it was reached. I directed the color bearer to march directly there, without halting; and, after getting out of fire, rode to the rear, and went round into the pike, and towards the front, looking for stragglers. I saw none; and, meeting the colors, found most of the regiment with them.

Captain Charles J. Rawling of the 1st West Virginia continued the account.

The order was given to fall back . . . in rear of the former position, where, being exposed to a withering fire of musketry and canister, was for a short time thrown into confusion; rallying . . . took position on Rude's Hill.

View of Bushong's Farm from Sigel's Hill, 1911. (Turner)

Federal Rear Area $\quad$ (F)

Walk about 60 yards west on the service road running parallel to the hedge row until it cuts through the hedge again. At this point, look to the north. The other five companies of the 1st West Virginia were on the knoll about 200 yards to the north of the hedge. General Sigel spent most of his time in this general area and farther toward the next stop. A staff officer's view of the situation was given by Sigel's Chief of Staff, Col. David H. Strother.

Sigel seemed in a state of excitement and rode here and there with Stahel and Moor, all jabbering in German. In his excitement, he seemed to forget his English entirely, and the purely American portion of his staff were totally useless to him. I followed him up and down until I got tired, and finding a group of his staff officers together near a battery, I stopped and got a drink of whiskey and a cracker which an artillery man gave me. These officers said the General had ordered them to remain there, but seeing him riding rapidly to the artillery position on our right, we started to join him. Just then the enemy appeared, advancing in two lines of battle extending unbroken along our whole front, while along the front of the cavalry a line of skirmishers was seen pushing forward. Our artillery immediately opened, all the guns firing with great rapidity. The enemy's artillery played chiefly on our cavalry which after making a few futile movements was totally withdrawn to the rear. The Rebel infantry continued to move in advance; in spite of our furious artillery fire their lines were steady and clean, no officers either mounted or on foot appearing among them. When within three hundred yards they began to yell as usual, and the musketry from both lines opened with great fury.

Overlook No. 1 $\quad$ (G)

Follow the service road about 40 yards from the hedge to Overlook Number One. Look south up the North Fork of the Shenandoah River. Shirley's Hill may be seen in the distance, half cleared–half wooded. The eastward bend of the river caused the 26th Virginia Battalion to be squeezed east itself, as it emerged from Indian Hollow. This caused it to form unintentionally in a line behind part of the 51st Virginia. You can see from here how the 26th and elements of the 51st were shielded by the terrain from most of the Federal fire. This was the area occupied by Company C, 34th Massachusetts, placed here to support the west flank of the guns and to bring rifle fire on Confederates advancing along the river's edge. The company was cut off and captured during the Federal withdrawal.

Walk directly east from the Overlook about 50 feet until you get a view of the guns to the south and US 11 north. General Sigel gave his version of events in this area.

There was an interruption of a few minutes, when the enemy's lines recoiled, and our men cheered; then the fire began again and lasted about thirty minutes; the enemy again

View of Shirley's Hill and north fork of Shenandoah from Sigel's Hill, 1911. (Turner)

charged, this time especially against our batteries; he came so near that Lieutenant Ephraim Chalfant of Carlin's battery rode up to me and said that he could not hold his position. I immediately ordered two companies of the 12th West Virginia to advance and protect the pieces, but to my surprise there was no disposition to advance; in fact, in spite of entreaties and reproaches, the men could not be moved an inch! At this moment, Major Meysenburg of my staff came up to me, and, to save the guns, I determined to make a counter-charge of the whole right wing, and requested him to transmit the order to Colonel Thoburn, who was not far from me toward the left.

I was chained to my advanced position on the right by a circumstance that is unpleasant to record. Desiring to know what was going on to the left, I soon turned to ride out of the smoke, and so gain a survey of the whole field. As I did so, the companies placed behind the batteries quickly rose from the ground and followed me, as if by command. I immediately turned around, brought them back to their position, and remained at my post. In spite of the seriousness of the situation, it seemed to me almost comical that a major general commanding a department and an "army" was condemned to the function of a "watchman." Then came the charge I ordered from our right. The disagreeable incident mentioned prevented me from performing an important duty.

Two miles to the north, Rude's Hill may be seen with the green-roofed, white-sided Cedar Grove Church at its base. Sigel could see the 28th and 116th Ohio forming around the church and directed the withdrawal toward it.

51

Battery Heights and Return (H)

Walk 30 yards south along the service road to the guns. You are in the area of Snow's Maryland Battery. Carlin's West Virginia Battery occupied the ground to the east, midway to the single tree and the gun symbolizing von Kleiser's position. The guns were set up about 14 feet from each other. To the south is the Field of Lost Shoes, behind which you can see the Bushong farm. Elements of the 26th and 51st Virginia charged across the field immediately to the front and left, capturing two of Carlin's guns left on the field. The VMI cadets charged farther to the left on a line from the farmhouse to von Kleiser's position. Farther east, north along US 11, Capt. Henry A. DuPont made the deployments mentioned earlier that eventually slowed the Confederate pursuit. As he related,

On the east side of that highway, the Union forces were in total rout and making for the rear in the wildest confusion—infantry and cavalry mingled with what was left of von Kleiser's battery.

No general officer was in sight, but I was at once pounced upon by a number of young and inexperienced staff officers who proceeded to give me (upon their own initiative but in the names of Generals Sigel or Stahel) the most absurd and contradictory orders with respect to putting the battery in position . . . but common sense, reinforced by eight years of continuous military instruction and military discipline, made it easy to reach an instant decision as to what ought to be done, and, although under fire for the first time in my life, I then and there made up my mind to ignore the conflicting instructions and to take such measures as seemed right and proper. In brief, I was compelled to act, and did act, upon my own judgment and of

course assumed all responsibility. This was the last that was seen of the staff officers in question, who evidently went promptly to the rear with the rest of Sigel's forces. . . . The battery was in the open and entirely without support, but the curtain of smoke which hung over the field prevented the Confederates from discovering this fact, and it seemed necessary to risk the loss of some of my guns in order to cover and protect the retreat of the Union troops. The leading platoon (two guns) under Second Lieutenant Charles Holman, was at once put in position close to the turnpike and on its right, or west side, and instantly opened fire. Taking advantage of this, I ordered the other four pieces to the rear, and riding back, put the center platoon, under First Sergeant S. D. Southworth, in position some 500 or 600 yards farther to the rear and in immediate proximity to the east side of the turnpike, with orders to open fire as soon as he was unmasked by Holman. Indicating a slight swell of the ground some 500 or 600 yards still farther to the rear, I also instructed Second Lieutenant B. F. Nash, commanding the left platoon, to go into position at that point. These dispositions, known in the tactics of that day as "retiring by echelon of platoons," consumed but a very few moments, when I galloped back to the front and remained with Lieutenant Holman's pieces which continued to fire with great rapidity and precision until we found ourselves entirely alone, with not a single Federal soldier in sight save the members of our own battery. Telling Holman that he had "to get out of this" and ordering him to go back at a gallop and take the best position he could find some 500 or 600 yards behind Nash's platoon.

From the guns, walk south along the service road; follow it west of the Bushong barn to its junction with another farm lane, turn east and walk past the Bushong House to the parking lot (.3

New Market Gap, looking east from the town. (Turner)

mile). As you walk along the road, notice the sharp drop of the ground to the west. This configuration protected the 26th Virginia Battalion and five companies of the 51st Virginia from the brunt of the Federal fire. Members of the 26th Virginia Battalion edged forward sufficiently to bring a withering fire on the Federal artillerymen and their teams from behind the ridge along which you are walking.

The 26th Virginia Battalion, 51st Virginia and 30th Virginia Battalion had become quite mixed by the time of the final charge. Major Peter Otey of the 30th, for example, commanded the three easternmost companies of the 51st Virginia as they moved across the boggy field.

If you have not done so earlier, drive .3 mile from the Bushong House to the museum to see it before completing your tour. We hope that this tour has clarified the events of the battle for you and that it has heightened your appreciation of the sacrifices made by the brave men and boys who fought here for the causes important to them. This is, indeed, a field of honor.

Notes